UNIVERSITY OF NORTH CAROLINA AT CHAPEL HILL
DEPARTMENT OF ROMANCE LANGUAGES

NORTH CAROLINA STUDIES
IN THE ROMANCE LANGUAGES AND LITERATURES

Founder: URBAN TIGNER HOLMES
Editor: STIRLING HAIG

Distributed by:

UNIVERSITY OF NORTH CAROLINA PRESS

CHAPEL HILL

North Carolina 27514

U.S.A.

NORTH CAROLINA STUDIES IN THE
ROMANCE LANGUAGES AND LITERATURES
Number 227

SOCIAL REALISM IN THE
ARGENTINE NARRATIVE

SOCIAL REALISM
IN THE
ARGENTINE NARRATIVE

BY

DAVID WILLIAM FOSTER

CHAPEL HILL

NORTH CAROLINA STUDIES IN THE ROMANCE
LANGUAGES AND LITERATURES
U.N.C. DEPARTMENT OF ROMANCE LANGUAGES

1986

Library of Congress Cataloging in Publication Data

Foster, David William.
  Social realism in the Argentine narrative.

  (North Carolina studies in the Romance languages and literatures; no. 227.)
  Includes bibliographical references.
  1. Argentine fiction — 20th century — History and criticism.   2. Realism
in literature.   3. Social problems in literature.   4. Soviet Union — History —
Revolution, 1917-1921 — Literature and the revolution.   I. Title.   II. Series.
PQ7703.F64   1986   863   86-8541
ISBN 0-8078-9231-9

ISBN 0-8078-9231-9

DEPÓSITO LEGAL: V. 1.317 - 1986   I.S.B.N. 84-599-1461-5

ARTES GRÁFICAS SOLER, S. A. - LA OLIVERETA, 28 - 46018 VALENCIA - 1986

Alguien debiera hablar, con toda su voz, de lo que pasa en este Buenos Aires oculto, que nadie ve; en este Buenos Aires hecho de sobras.

(Miguel Ángel Speroni, *La puerta grande; aventura y desventura de Buenos Aires; novela* [Buenos Aires: Editorial Claridad, 1947], p. 22.)

Toda la literatura rusa, ahora, está absorbida por un solo pensamiento: construcción. La nuestra no puede ser absorbida más que por la idea contraria: destrucción.

(Elías Castelnuovo, *Vidas proletarias (escenas de la lucha obrera).* [Buenos Aires: Editorial Victoria, 1934], p. 19.)

¡Siglo veinte, cambalache
problemático y febril...
El que no llora no mama
y el que no afana es un gil!

(Enrique Santos Discépolo, "Cambalache" [tango, 1935].)

CONTENTS

I. INTRODUCTION

> Su gran escuela [del artista], entonces, no puede
> ser otra que la escuela de la revolución. Su gran
> maestro, el proletariado. Su gran fuente de trabajo
> y de inspiración, la lucha que sostiene en contra de
> sus opresores. Y, por último, su de ser y de vivir
> en comunión con él: porque de la emancipación de
> la clase trabajadora depende su propia emancipación,
> la emancipación del arte y de la cultura, su vida pre-
> sente y su porvenir. (Castelnuovo 1935: 191.)

> Por ello, y a pesar de todo, esas novelas de la
> izquierda durante la "década infame", continuaron
> siendo el cuerpo vivo de nuestra literatura. Mucho
> mejor orientadas que los trabajos de los intuicionis-
> tas, ellas pagaron el duro precio de pretender el ca-
> mino de la integración con el pueblo, en momentos
> de atonía general de la sociedad argentina. (Portan-
> tiero: 127-28.)

This monograph proposes to undertake a reassessment of the
novel of social realism in Argentina during the years 1930-1950.
There is wide recognition that the Argentine novel during the twentieth century is one of the major literary forces in Latin America, and
novels by contemporary writers like Julio Cortázar and Manuel Puig
have, through the extensive foreign translations of their works, joined
Jorge Luis Borges's short stories in achieving a high degree of international prominence. The twentieth century in Argentina has been a
period of intensive intellectual and artistic activity, and the novel is
one of the principal manifestations of that activity.

Nevertheless, recent critical attention has tended to focus almost
exclusively on works written during the sixties and seventies, with
little but sporadic interest shown in developments between the literary

vanguard of the 1920s and novels of the last twenty years. Although
there is a considerable bibliography of criticism on Eduardo Mallea,
one of the key figures of the 1940s in the novel, interest in his
writings has waned; the same may be said of other novelists who
flourished between 1920 and 1960. There is no question that international interest in the works of more recent writers has stimulated
critical emphasis on their works and a tendency to disregard earlier
novelists. In part, this interest in production since 1960 has coincided
with the American and European "discovery" of Latin America, and
in part it owes itself to the correspondences between current works,
the international literary scene, and prevailing critical models that
place a premium on magical realism, ironic modes of narrative, structural complexity and ambiguity, and foregrounded language in the
Joycean, modernist tradition.

Critics are deeply divided as to whether or not tags like *nueva
narrativa latinoamericana/hispanoamericana* or the "boom" describe
a coherent movement and, if so, whether or not that movement
possesses sociocultural validity. Whatever one's position in this
matter is, it would be difficult to deny that the mid-sixties saw
significant modifications in the priorities for fiction writing in Latin
America. One of the consequences of such a modification is a reconsid-
eration, on the part of both writers and critics, of the criteria of
preceding literary programs. This is particularly true in the case of
social realism. Since novelists like Julio Cortázar, Gabriel García
Márquez, Mario Vargas Llosa — all pivotal figures of Latin American
fiction since the sixties — have been concerned with social problems,
it is only natural that we see the attempt to define the differences
between their writing and the principles to which the social realists
adhered.

Ángel Rama, who devoted considerable attention to the analysis
of the sociocultural issues associated with the novel in Latin America,
underscores the way in which the social realists, despite their commitment to proletarian issues and specifically regional problems (pace
those whose first allegiance was to the Communist Internationale),
continued in their writing to subscribe to the conventions of the
bourgeois novel:

> La novela social latinoamericana de los treinta ni siquiera
> se planteó este asunto como un problema, no discutió si
> estaba operando con una de las formas predilectas de la cul-

tura occidental burguesa, limitándose a violentarla para que aceptara una ideología que respondía a las orientaciones de un pensamiento de izquierda (en el cual se mezclaba liberalismo, progresismo, tímidos escarceos marxistas) sin modificar demasiado notoriamente sus formas, apenas si simplificándolas en un régimen más marcadamente denotativo y lógicoracional. La beligerancia que ese pensamiento demostró en cambio respecto a las formas posteriores de la novela vanguardista, a las que interpretó como manifestaciones de la desintegración burguesa en el período imperialista, no la ejerció respecto a las formas anteriores de la novela correspondientes a la etapa de triunfo y expansión de la burguesía europea. Las aceptó pasivamente y ni siquiera las utilizó irónicamente como lo hiciera uno de los grandes epígonos del siglo XIX, Thomas Mann. En tal comportamiento es posible discernir una secreta conexión cultural, la continuidad de una determinada concepción de lo real y de las formas literarias para traducirla, que sólo acepta variaciones de grado y no de sustancia, apuntando así a las contradicciones que presentan los nuevos grupos sociales que, sin embargo, pertenecen a la misma pauta cultural. (Rama: 211-212)

It is undeniable that earlier novelistic production, while it may manifest traces of the modernist aesthetics (the early poetry and stories of Borges are, of course, the prime example of the literary vanguard in Argentina), seems pale and unaccomplished when compared to acclaimed masterpieces of the last twenty years; the same is true of more current examples of political and social commitment. Characterized — as was the international production of social realist fiction — by an innocent belief in the power of the word and in the honest writer's ability to portray in a satisfying documentary fashion the structure of social reality, the fiction published between 1930 and 1950 in Argentina is routinely denigrated as artistically stunted: facile plots, unreflecting narrators, and journalistic language are the essential features of these efforts and the main reason for their perceived inadequacy as narrative art. The reliance of the social realist novel on the outworn conventions of the bourgeois novel and naturalism had already been underscored in the thirties by the American critic Harold Strauss:

> Misguided in technique and, for the most part, ineffectual, the proletarian novelists nonetheless have held to a sound literary purpose. How they were trapped and defeated

by their addiction to photographic realism is an ironic tale. [...] The proletarian novel, as we knew it a few years ago, bore within itself the seeds of its own destruction because it sprang not from the vision of the proletariat, or of society in general, as a creative force but from despair and disillusionment. It invented no new methods of its own, but adopted the decadent technique of photographic realism. [...]

The mere description of this method already makes clear the extent to which writers who use it have turned their backs upon the novelist's onetime mission of clarifying and ordering human experience. For, implicit in the rejection of the right to judge behavior, one perceives the perverse notion that chaos is more profoundly meaningful than order. Those very novelists, the proletarians, who presumedly wished to survey the orderly pattern of stress and strain in society, by a curious process of rationalization have pledged themselves to the disorderly technique of photographic realism. (Strauss: 361-362)

It is in the context of these diverse reservations about the accomplishments of social realism that the present study is undertaken.

Social realism as defined by this study may be properly limited to a group of authors who wrote in the 1930s and 1940s, inspired in various ways by the Russian revolution, Soviet communism, international Marxism, and the need to respond critically and in a denunciatory fashion to the various mechanisms of repression and the frustration of personal and collective aspirations during the period. It is a period marked by the violent military takeover of September 1930. Jesús Méndez, in his outstanding study on intellectual movements in Argentina in the early part of this century, characterizes the feelings of writers and artists after the Uriburu coup in the following terms:

In spite of some institutional advances in the intellectual and cultural arena in Argentina in the early 1930s, widespread individual disenchantment existed among intellectuals. One of the reasons for the grim atmosphere was the political and economic panorama in the country after the September Revolution. During the previous 50 years, Argentine intellectuals had been praising their country on the basis of two trends, the unprecedented economic growth and prosperity, and the political stability along democratic lines. These two characteristics became the basis for the formation of the Argentine "national mythology," in the absence of a long cultural and historical tradition. The combination of the world economic depression and the overthrow of the constitutionally elected president by a military coup seemed to undermine the foundations of the nation. In this regard, the literature of pessimism and disenchantment of Argentine intellectuals in the 1930s reflected the general discontent and disillusionment of the Argentine population as a whole.

Yet, one must go further than the mere reflection of the feelings of the general population to explain the depths of despair of Argentine intellectuals in the 1930s. The crisis of 1930 certainly exacerbated intellectual pessimism in Argentina, but it did not cause it. The roots of disillusionment ran deeper than the political and economic events of 1930. The intellectual expressions of the 1930s are part of an increasing alienation which had its origins in the early years of the century. The crisis of the 1930s underscored the state of individual impotence which had overtaken Argentine intellectuals as a result of their overdependence on patronage, both from the government and the oligarchy, and their spiritual reliance on inspiration from abroad, not only for ideas but also for intellectual models of professional behavior. The absence of self-generated parameters of behavior led to a deep crisis of individual identity when the veneer of national stability vanished. (Méndez: 282-84)

Although the limits of the group of writers studied here are vaguely marked, there is no question that they represent a commitment to social questions arising from the situation of Argentina in the 1930s Méndez described, in addition to their correspondences with general issues in the Latin American and Western novel of the period. The difficulty of defining the limits of a topic like social realism is evident in the scope of the works studied by Ralph B. Kite in his doctoral dissertation. While it is abundantly clear that he is examining the same movement or phenomenon as the present study, the works of Argentine literature that he analyzes are basically all from the 1950s; several are from the late years of the decade. As a consequence, except for a passing reference to Alfredo Varela's *El río oscuro* and some comments on Bernardo Verbitsky, but with reference to his 1957 *Villa miseria también es América,* the writers featured in the chapters that follow are not included in Kite's study. One surmises that Kite found Mexican, Ecuadorian, and Chilean works of the 1930s and 1940s more illustrative of the principles of social realism, which he examines in detail with the goal of establishing the clear links with the Russian postulates. It is of little consequence for the purposes of my investigation whether or not this is true. The important point to be made is that Kite and I have not duplicated each other's efforts.

However, it is important to recognize that the term social realism, a term that derives from Russian-inspired beliefs about the function of literature in a revolutionary socialist society (Hart, Ermolaev), has been used by a number of critics either to define a general emphasis on social concerns throughout the history of Latin American fiction (González y Contreras, Losada) and to stress the priority of such a commitment among contemporary novelists, as opposed to the modernist or formalist tendencies of the putatively dependent *nueva narrativa* and its derivations (Aguirre), or to articulate a call for an unqualified supremacy of realism in fiction (Portantiero, Aguirre, Bignami). Clearly, all such positions owe much to the writers of the 1930s and 1940s, especially as concerns the imperative to deal in a forthright fashion with the social concerns and to represent explicitly the texture of the daily life of the "people" of Latin America without the mediating — and, therefore, presumedly confusing — structures or techniques of modernist/formalist writing.

By contrast, the present investigation is motivated by the belief that the work of the social realists cannot be written off as an unimpressive component of Argentine fiction. In the first place, the social realists are the direct heirs of the Boedo group of committed writers who in the late 1920s shared the enthusiasm of the members of the modernist literary vanguard for the possibility of reforming Argentine letters; indeed, there was considerable crossbreeding between the two groups. Nevertheless, and despite its proletarian commitment and its focus on the plight of immigrant groups and oppressed workers, the so-called Boedo group of writers, as Carlos R. Giordano makes clear, cannot be confused with the writers who emerge under the aegis of the subsequent left: "Para ser más exactos, la literatura de izquierda no debe confundirse con el boedismo, una de sus formas (y desde la perspectiva actual, una de las más cuestionables), a pesar de que el boedismo influye sobre mucha de la posterior literatura de izquierda" (Giordano, 966).

In the second place, one of the major literary figures of the late twenties and thirties, Roberto Arlt, has received extensive reevaluation in recent years. Although his work does not jibe with the canon of the social realists — in fact, his rediscovery is based on the ways in which he anticipates the new Latin American narrative — his fiction (as well as his journalism and his theater) deals with the harsh social realities of Argentine life, and it is difficult to believe that the rich texture of his brilliant, if often curiously flawed and fragmentary, work did not exercise a direct influence on the social realists.

But the most important reason for undertaking a reevaluation of the social realists is the change in current narrative aesthetics and critical theories. Latin American critics speak of the period of the "postboom": the collapse of the artistic and social enthusiasms of the sixties and the realization that social revolution has been fatefully stalled and that literature is not, in fact, a revolutionary force, despite fervent beliefs to the contrary. Moreover, the grandiose mythopoetic versions of Latin American socioculture by the principal names of the boom may have served less to elaborate a density of meaning for Latin America than to serve up ineffectual romantic epics. Finally, critical reluctance to continue to sustain distinctions between art and nonart and to accord priority to rich "poetic" languages has encouraged attention to contemporary writers like Manuel Puig, whose novels reveal an insistent intertextuality with the detritus of the mass media and popular culture, the banes of mythopoeic writing. Viewed from this perspective, the writings of the social realists may not be as flat or uncreative as critics have been wont to assert and the nonliterary features that have most disturbed critics may, after all, constitute a valid from of novelistic writing.

By the mid-1950s, Perón's government, while it had already begun to totter, had coopted and institutionalized many of the issues that had been of concern first to the Boedo writers and then to the social realists. The non-Soviet left (Perón persecuted all forms of the left, as he did any group or individual that questioned his programs) had, inspired by the intellectual currents in Europe after World War II, begun to seek new models for the commitment to radical social change. One of the major publications of the non-Soviet left during this period in Argentina is *Contorno* (1953-1959.) Among its many concerns was a severe revisionism toward the paragons of the Argentine literary tradition, maintaining a stance that was in diametric opposition to *Sur*.

However, *Contorno*'s "parricidal" line of inquiry (to use the phrase coined by Emir Rodríguez Monegal to describe this stance)

extended also to other varieties of writing that were felt to be dis-
consonant with the goals of the journal. Such was the case of the
social realists, several of whose representative writers were dismissed
by Noé Jitrik (1955) as "los comunistas" because of their allegedly
outmoded identification with realism as defined by the Soviet cultural
commissars: "La técnica que emplean —1943 a 1955— es la que
corresponde al más ingenuo realismo, a un naturalismo cuyo mayor
sentido, precario, se dió en la época en que la mentalidad burguesa
obtenía sus más íntimas y más caras satisfacciones" (p. 48). Jitrik
proceeds to analyze works by four authors (Juan José Manauta, Leónidas Barletta, Álvaro Yunque, and Alfredo Varela) as representative
of this unfortunate narrative endeavor. Because of their affiliation
with international social realism, these authors are seen to have little
contribution to Argentine literature: Varela's *El río oscuro* is dismissed as not even "una novela americana" (p. 50).

One could argue that many of the writers promoted by *Contorno*
and by Jitrik in the 1950s, with the notable exception of David Viñas,
did not achieve much of a reputation (see Jitrik 1959). But this
would be as unfair as Jitrik is in excoriating Varela and company
for an enthusiasm that, in its day, made both social and artistic
sense. But it should be obvious that Jitrik did echo well the critical
assessment that led to the margination of the social realists in Argentina, a margination that was to be even more acute with the emergence of the "nueva narrativa" in the 1960s.

My goal, however, is not to revindicate the social realists of
Argentina, nor is it to prove that there existed a more coherent
movement than the fragmentary treatments of the literary histories
seem to provide. I have deliberately cast wide the net of my definitions, not so much so as to have a great range of works to analyze,
as legitimate a critical objective as this may be. Rather, I have wanted
to be sensitive to the dangers of defining Latin American literary
movements exclusively in terms of American and European categories
and to recognize the simple fact that adherents in Argentina of social
realism, of the proletarian novel, or of writing of revolutionary commitment may well produce varieties of literature that do not match
prior definitions very well. By concerning myself with those works
that focus on forgotten elements of society — whether oppressed agricultural and factory workers, exploited secretaries, children, and
assorted social misfits — and that assume a narrative tone of denun-

ciation and revelation of nonelite social realities, I feel that a significant group of narratives written during a turbulent period of Argentine social history has been identified.

A revindication of these works would set out to demonstrate how they are in someway better, more structurally original, or deserving of a greater reputation than they currently enjoy. Of course, writers like Bernardo Kordon, Elías Castelnuovo, Raúl Scalabrini Ortiz possess secure places in the Argentine literary canon, despite the abiding paucity of sustained critical analysis of their writing. Other writers have tended to become overlooked because of shifting cultural or literary priorities. The purpose of literary scholarship cannot really be to argue that texts are better than various groups of readers have deemed them to be. The mere existence of literary or cultural texts is sufficient justification for their study, and the operation of critical analysis is one of providing them with a context or set of contexts that expands their meaningfulness as semiological structures and enables us to read them in new lights. If a new reading contributes to a greater appreciation for a text, then in some indirect way we have contributed to revaluing, if not exactly revindicating it. It is my opinion that the texts that I have brought together under the rubric of social realism do not need to be recognized as the equal of the writings of Borges or Julio Cortázar. Of greater importance is affording them adequate critical examination so that their place in Argentine literary history is better grasped.

Thus, the reassessment of the social realist novels will undertake to study the coherence of narrative perspectives, the legitimacy of stylistic registers, and the conventions of plot structures. For example, stylistic registers (one of the concerns of the study) appear to reflect a contradictory pattern. On the one hand and presumably as a consequence of the journalistic livelihood of most of the writers involved, there is a legitimate concern for the authentic mirroring of the texture of colloquial Argentine Spanish, particularly of the nonelite classes. Yet, by contrast, these writers often felt the need to dignify their noble, exploited innocents by attributing to them a sort of "Volkspoesie" lyricism. Of fundamental importance is the evaluation of the interplay between these two stylistic norms.

Also of particular interest is a consideration of the resonance provided by strategies for allusions to Argentine social history: after all, these were novels written to influence social thinking, and any density of meaning they may possess will depend essentially on such resonance. The working assumption of the investigation has been that the novels possess a literary interest more important than the merely historical. Indeed, social realism in the 1930-1950 period in Argentina needs to be recognized for its ambitious goals: a massive rethinking and fictional rewriting of Argentine sociocultural history. No other literary creators in Spanish America matched the prose fiction writers in Argentina at this time in the idealistic goals of their enterprise and the volume of resulting writings, no matter how flawed we may now view their enterprise to have been.

The choice of the year 1930 as the terminus ab quo for this study is hardly an arbitrary one, and it does not reflect the literary historian's desire to segment the unending flow of texts into neat compartments based on the span of a decade or a generation. The same is true of the choice of 1950 to close the period. The military revolution of September 1930 triggered a far-reaching alteration in Argentine social and cultural consciousness. The end of the liberal/ radical democratic period and the emergence of authoritarian rule and the subsequent period of disorderly institutional continuity in Argentina stimulated precisely the sort of interpretation and revisionism characteristic of social realism. By the same token, the collapse of Peronismo and the need for the left — at least the younger generation of which Adolfo Prieto speaks — to define a position at variance with the social programs and proletarian ideology of Peronismo meant a turning to the newer forms of post-World War II fiction being pursued in the United States and Europe that underscored the passing of the particular focuses of the social realists.

Fernando Alonso and Arturo Rezzano have studied the continuity of an interest in social issues in Argentine letters (see also Arístides Gandolfi Herrero [Álvaro Yunque]), and, if such a commitment were all that were of interest to this investigation, there would be no special advantage to identifying the loose program of the thirties and forties. It is for this reason that the fact that the Boedo writers of the 1920s (the name refers to a street in a working-class section of Buenos Aires frequented by proletarian writers) were concerned with social issues overlaps with but does not duplicate the concerns of the social realists. As Elías Castelnuovo has pointed out in one of the programmatic statements of the period, the Boedo novelists (whom he neither identifies by name nor tags specifically with reference to the famous street) were essentially inspired by a sort of romantic anarchism that impeded their grasping the overall social dynamics of the situations and individuals they chose to portray in fictional terms:

> [P]ese a la sinceridad que lo distinguía y al deseo evidente de reflejar en sus obras las aspiraciones de las capas más oprimidas de la población, los propósitos de este grupo se frustraron, a menudo, lamentablemente, merced a su falta de captación política para crear un arte concretamente revolucionario. Fué, así, que su producción, sin haber sido nunca histórica, pasó rápidamente a la historia. [...] El mal de ese grupo era un mal específicamente anárquico. Aunque, como decimos, estaban todos juntos, concentrados literariamente en el mismo lugar, cada uno por su cuenta, después, sobre las líneas generales del dogma colectivo, se elaboraba para su particular recreo, otro dogma individual. Al examen objetivo y dialéctico, se oponía el examen subjetivo y crónico. (Castelnuovo 1934: 7-8)

One could recognize in this description the character of Remo Erdosain in Roberto Arlt's *Los siete locos* (1929) and *Los lanzallamas* (1931), as well as the writings of Roberto Mariani, Leónidas Barletta, and (on occasion) Enrique González Tuñón, among others. It is possible to question the degree to which all of the works examined in this study — for example, Castelnuovo's own *Larvas* — comply with the imperative to substitute revolutionary fervor for anarchic lamentations over the miserable social lot of the proletariat, to replace simply the chronicling of despair and degradation with the portrayal of the beneficent action of the proletariat in its own behalf. But the important point to be made is the change in perspective that Castelnuovo articulates on behalf of the recognition of a distinctive literary program.

Finally, it is important to note that the existence of a distinctive group of social realist writers is not universally recognized by scholarship on Argentine fiction. Neither Juan Carlos Ghiano, Germán García, nor Carmelo M. Bonet recognizes such a category. One may attribute such a silence in part to the desire to eschew "foreign" categories for Argentine literature, particularly when such categories derive from beliefs essentially alien to the interests of the academic community: the Marxist-Communist-Soviet inspiration of many of the concerns of the social realists, from Elías Castelnuovo's and

Alfredo Varela's explicit identification to the weaker affiliations of other writers, undoubtedly accounts for the unwillingness of scholars writing during antileftist governments like Peronismo (García) and subsequent military regimes (Ghiano and Bonet). Thus, Ghiano's comment on the social content of Varela's *El río oscuro* really means his sense of a hostile natural environment and only obliquely the concerns of an exploited rural proletariat: "Otros novelistas, al acercarse al ámbito rural, se relacionan con preocupados sociales de otros países de nuestra América. Seres acosados por una naturaleza huraña, cuando no enemiga, patrones rapaces y titánicos, explotación cruel del trabajo humilde, son temas que uniforman muchas de las historias, no siempre elaboradas literariamente. [...] Las dimensiones de poderío, inmensidad y salvajismo de la naturaleza estrechan a los hombres [de *El río oscuro*] que trabajan en esa zona; la inclemencia es la nota dominante en sus actos" (Ghiano: 12-13; no explanation is given for the qualification "no siempre elaboradas literariamente"). These comments certainly do not reflect the sentiment of rebellion that is the whole rationale for the story of the main character of the novel.

Another factor that may explain the lack of interest of these literary historians in identifying a social realist component of the Argentine novel is the simple fact that many of the authors and works that constitute such a canon are simply ignored. For a critic like Ghiano, the major points of reference for the 1940s must be Eduardo Mallea and Leopoldo Marechal (who was primarily a poet, although his Joycean *Adán Buenoayres* [1948 but begun in the 1920s] is undoubtedly the most ambitious — or most pretentious — fictional work of the period). As a consequence, the bulk of the writers of concern to the present investigation deserve only a passing, if any, reference. There can, therefore, be little question that the literary tastes represented by a segment of Argentine academic criticism led either to ignoring social realist writing or to downplaying its importance. The fact that the works were published and that critical scholarship exists on individual texts or the work of specific authors attests to a response among Argentine readers, despite the sketchy representation of these works in comprehensive literary histories. Only Pedro Orgambide and Roberto Yahni, in their *Enciclopedia de la literatura argentina,* and Jorge B. Rivera in his fascicule in the *Capítulo* series of the Centro Editor de América

Latina — both of which are fundamentally revisionist contributions — provide an adequate characterization of the social realist authors from the Uriburu coup d'état to the fall of Perón. It is as an elaboration on this revisionist perspective that recognizes the importance of these writers and their specific project, as well as its derivations that are less programmatically committed than doctrinaire social realists would insist, that the present study is undertaken.

A few comments concerning the scope and organization of this study. I have chosen to concentrate attention on the narrative of social realism. Although there are considerable examples in other genres, there can be little doubt the greatest investment of these writers, in accord with the prominence of fiction in contemporary literature and society, was in the area of the novel and the short story. I have analyzed in a separate monograph the dramatic production in Argentina during the period examined in this study, and an investigation of poetry would necessarily provide a more global picture. Certainly, the texts of the tango, that Argentine cultural artifact *par excellence* that combines lyrics, music, and dance, would figure prominently in a discussion of contributions to social realism made by poets. The sheer vastness of Argentine literature during this period, in part an extension of the growth of writing during the earlier vanguard or modernist period but also simply because an immense output of creative writing is a hallmark of Argentine culture, encourages one, in a study devoted to examining specific texts in detail, to limit the scope to one dominant genre.

However, a belief in the virtues of structural asymmetry has lead me to indulge in one exception. Raúl Scalabrini Ortiz's essay, *El hombre que está solo y espera,* contributed perhaps the most prominent cultural figure of the writing of this period, the Hombre de Corrientes y Esmeralda. In his essay, Scalabrini Ortiz alludes to his intention to publish a work of fiction based on the themes elucidated with respect to the Hombre de Corrientes y Esmeralda. Unfortunately, such a novel was never forthcoming, and it is by way of recognizing both the importance of the human type postulated by Scalabrini Ortiz and the probable significance a novelized embodiment of the type would have enjoyed that I have included an analysis of *El hombre que está solo y espera.*

This study is organized with the intention of describing the importance of the works examined in detail in constituting a coherent pattern of social realist narrative in Argentina. The first section, "Defining the Context," deals with four novels and Scalabrini Ortiz's essay. These novels all provide major examples of the way in which Argentine society, as a complex mosaic of human preoccupations and suffering, is viewed by these writers. Bernardo Kordon and Leónidas Barletta examine a representative array of individuals and concerns, and it is in this context that Scalabrini Ortiz sketches the portrait of what he considers to be the period's most human type. Of considerable importance in a characterization of the Argentine urban society of the period is the presence of vast numbers of as yet unassimilated immigrants, and the two major blocks of immigrants, Italians and Jews, are portrayed by Luis María Albamonte and José Rabinovich, respectively.

If the first group of writers may be examined with emphasis on their characterization of the situations and life styles of the period, in "Toward a Critical Consciousness," a group of works are studied that focus on individuals who develop a fundamentally critical consciousness toward their society, and issues of alienation, margination, and the destruction of the human spirit are provided by Bernardo Verbitsky (who typically deals with Jewish immigrants now assimilated into the mainstream of Argentine society though spiritually alienated from it), Max Dickmann (a writer of Jewish origins but whose array of characters are not ethnically defined), and Carlos Ruiz Daudet.

The final section of this study, *Proletarians, the Oppressed, and the Forgotten,* analyzes works in which the social realist message is most aggressively present. This message may take the form of sociological documentariness, as in the case of fiction dealing with the oppression of children (Elías Castelnuovo and Álvaro Yunque), or it may detail specific issues of exploitation, as in the case of Alfredo Varela (agricultural workers in the jungle) or Josefina Marpons (the urban lower middle class). A novel by Juan Goyanarte serves as a sort of synthesis of the overall margination and destruction of an Everyman figure within the context of the global dysfunction of society of concern to the social realists. This principle of organization corresponds to my interest in examining a highly selective inventory of works in detail rather than simply in classifying the very extensive total production of the period.

It will be immediately apparent, from the nature of the works discussed and extrinsic information the reader may have about these authors, that there is an almost exclusive emphasis on what can be loosely called "leftist" writers. This is only natural, since social realism is customarily understood to be a cultural manifestation of the commitment to the model of the Russian revolution and its ideological derivations. There are, to be sure, considerable differences from one writer to another, and, were this study more historical or sociological in orientation, the extraliterary political beliefs and activities of these authors would play a more prominent role in my analyses. Suffice it to say that individuals are included who are respected names of the leftist establishment (Barletta, Castelnuovo, Dickmann, Ruíz Daudet, Varela, Yunque), while someone like Albamonte has been identified with Peronista populism. Marpons and Rabinovich are brought into the orbit by the features of the works examined without my being able neatly to classify them in terms of political ideology. Kordon currently professes an anti-Soviet but pro-China commitment. Verbitsky and Scalabrini Ortiz typify the general leftist, populist attitude of writers of the period, rather than the aggressive, pro-Soviet stance that one is wont to identify with "high" or classical social realism (e.g., Castelnuovo in his programmatic writing in the 1930s). That my scope has been a fairly generous one mediates between the need to recognize a social realist commitment among Argentine writers of the period and the need not to force them into molds dictated by European or other foreign schemata.

Social realism was closely circumscribed by the events of the period, and, toward establishing the social and historical parameters of the works discussed, I have appended to this introduction a chronology for the 1930-1955 period.

BIBLIOGRAPHY

Aaron, Daniel. *Writers on the Left.* New York: Avon, 1965.

Agosti, Héctor P. *Defensa del realismo*; 3rd ed. Buenos Aires: Editorial Lautaro, 1962. Orig. 1945.

Aguirre, Mirta. "Realismo y realismo socialista." *L/L,* Nos. 7-8 (1976-1977), 3-37.

Alonso, Fernando Pedro, and Arturo Ressano. *Novela y sociedad argentinas.* Buenos Aires: Paidós, 1971.

Barletta, Leónidas. "Gente de Boedo." *Testigo,* No. 2 (1966), 18-22.

Beach, Joseph Warren. *American Fiction 1920-1940.* New York: Atheneum, 1972.

Bignami, Ariel. *Notas para la polémica sobre el realismo.* Buenos Aires: Galerna, 1969.

Bogantes, Claudio, and Ursula Kuhlmann. "El surgimiento del realismo social en Centroamérica 1930-1970." *Revista de crítica literaria latinoamericana,* No. 17 (1983), 39-64.

Bogardus, Ralph F. and Fred Hobson, eds. *Literature at the Barricades: The American Writer in the 1930s.* University: University of Alabama Press, 1982.

Bonet, Carmelo M. "La novela." In Rafael Alberto Arrieta, *Historia de la literatura argentina* (Buenos Aires: Ediciones Peuser, 1958-1960), IV, 131-284.

Borello, Rodolfo A. "Novela e historia; la visión fictiva del período peronista (1944-1955) en las letras argentinas." *Anales de literatura hispanoamericana,* No. 8 (1980), 29-72.

Castelnuovo, Elías. *El arte y las masas; ensayos sobre una nueva teoría de la actividad estética.* Buenos Aires: Colección Claridad, 1935.

———. "Introducción." In his *Vidas proletarias (escenas de la lucha proletaria).* Buenos Aires: Editorial Victoria, 1934), pp. 5-26.

Echevarra, Evelio. "Bolshevism and the Spanish American Social Novel." *Latin American Literary Review,* No. 8 (1976), 89-95.

Ermolaev, Herman. *Soviet Literary Theories, 1917-1934: the Genesis of Socialist Realism.* New York: Octagon Books, 1977. Orig. 1963.

Foster, David William. *The Argentine Teatro Independiente (1930-1955).* York, SC: Spanish Literature Publications, forthcoming.

———. *Currents in the Contemporary Argentine Novel.* Columbia: University of Missouri Press, 1975.

Gandolfi Herrero, Arístides (Álvaro Yunque). *La literatura social en la Argentina.* Buenos Aires: Claridad, 1941.

García, Germán. *La novela argentina; un itinerario.* Buenos Aires: Editorial Sudamericana, 1952.

Ghiano, Juan Carlos. *La novela argentina contemporánea, 1940-1960.* Buenos Aires: Ministerio de Relaciones Exteriores y Culto, 1964.

Giordano, Carlos R. *Boedo y el tema social.* Buenos Aires: Centro Editor de América Latina, 1967. *Capítulo: la historia de la literatura argentina,* No. 40.

González y Contreras, Gilberto. "Aclaraciones a la novela social americana." *Revista iberoamericana,* No. 12 (1943), 403-418.

Guerra-Cunningham, Lucía. "El realismo socialista en la novela chilena de la generación de 1938." *Cuadernos americanos,* No. 209 (1976), 190-205.

Hart, Henry, ed. *The American Writers' Congress.* New York: International Publishers, 1935.

Heise, Karl H. "*El Grupo de Guayaquil*", *arte y técnica de sus novelas sociales.* Madrid: Playor, 1975.

Hernández Arregui, Juan José. *Imperialismo y cultura; la política en la inteligencia argentina.* Buenos Aires: Amerinda, 1957. 3rd ed., 1973.

Jameson, Fredric. *The Political Unconscious: Narrative as Socially Symbolic Act.* Ithaca: Cornell University Press, 1981.

Jitrik, Noé. "Los comunistas (Manauta, Barletta, Yunque, Varela)." *Contorno,* Nos. 5-6 (1955), 48-51.

———. *Seis novelistas argentinos de la nueva promoción.* Mendoza: Cuadernos de Versión, 1959.

Justo, Liborio (Lobodón Garra, pseud.). *Literatura argentina y expresión argentina.* Buenos Aires: Rescate, 1976.

Klein, Marcus. *Foreigners: The Making of American Literature 1900-1940.* Chicago: University of Chicago Press, 1981.

Losada, Alejandro. "Rasgos específicos del realismo social en la América hispánica." *Revista iberoamericana,* Nos. 108-109 (1979), 413-442.

———. "El surgimiento del realismo social en la literatura de América latina." *I&L, Ideologies & Literature,* No. 11 (1979), 20-55.

Méndez, Jesús. "Argentine Intellectuals in the Twentieth Century, 1900-1943." Unpublished Ph.D. dissertation, University of Texas at Austin, 1980.

Orgambide, Pedro, and Roberto Yahni, eds. *Enciclopedia de la literatura argentina.* Buenos Aires: Editorial Sudamericana, 1970.

Paita, Jorge A., ed. *Argentina 1930-1960.* Buenos Aires: Sur, 1961.

Pearson, Lon. *Nicomedes Guzmán: Proletarian Author in Chile's Literary Generation of 1938.* Columbia: University of Missouri Press, 1976.

Ponce, Aníbal. *Humanismo burgués y humanismo proletario.* México, D.F.: Editorial América, 1938.

Portuondo, Juan Carlos. *Realismo y realidad en la narrativa argentina.* Buenos Aires: Procyón, 1961.

Prieto, Adolfo. *Borges y la nueva generación.* Buenos Aires: Letras Universitarias, 1954.

Rama, Ángel. *Transculturación narrativa en América latina.* México, D.F.: Siglo XX, 1982.

Rideout, Walter B. *The Radical Novel in the United States: 1900-1954; Some Interrelations of Literature and Society.* New York: Hill and Wang, 1966.

Rivera, Jorge B. *Panorama de la novela argentina: 1930-1955.* Buenos Aires: Centro Editor de América Latina, 1981. *Capítulo: la historia de la literatura argentina,* No. 86.

Rodríguez Monegal, Emir. *El juicio de los parricidas.* Buenos Aires: Deucalión, 1956.

Rosser, Harry L. *Conflict and Transition in Rural Mexico: The Fiction of Social Realism.* Boston: Crossroads Press, 1980.

Sebreli, Juan José. *Buenos Aires, vida cotidiana y alienación;* 15a ed. Buenos Aires: Ediciones Siglo Veinte, 1979.

Strauss, Harold. "Realism in the Proletarian Novel." *Yale Review,* 28 (1938), 360-374.

Verdugo, Iber H. "Testimonio y denuncia en la novela argentina." *Aportes,* No. 8 (1968), 38-87.

Viñas, David. *Literatura argentina y realidad política;* ed. rev. Buenos Aires: Jorge Álvarez, 1971-75. Orig. 1964.

APPENDIX: CHRONOLOGY

1930　The right-wing Liga Patriótica Argentina demands the resignation of Radical president Hipólito Yrigoyen; on June 6 the army revolts against the government, and on June 10 General José Félix Uriburu assumes the presidency in the name of the military.

1931　The Radical party is excluded from provincial elections, and the government refuses to recognize elections in the province of Buenos Aires. Publication of Raúl Scalabrini Ortiz's *El hombre que está solo y espera* and Elías Castelnuovo's *Larvas*.

1932   Agustín P. Justo, elected at the end of 1931 in the so-called Fórmula de la Concordancia, assumes the presidency. By decree, the five-day work week goes into effect, the *sábado inglés*).

1933   The Senate approves the Roca-Runciman pact acquiescing to Great Britain's demands for preferential trade and economic provisions. The pact has often been considered one of the most scandalous official acts of the period, a veritable touchstone of the Década Infame. Approval of various worker benefits, including paid vacations, sick leave, death benefits, and the like.

1934   Investigation into irregularities in the livestock and meat packing industry. An international Eucharistic Congress is held in Buenos Aires, a tribute to the conservative Catholicism dominating public life.

1935   The Radical party once again allowed to participate in national elections. Senator Bordabehere is assassinated in the Senate chambers. Founding of FORJA (Fuerza Orientadora Radical de la Joven Argentina), a group for political and social renovation. Publication of Max Dickmann's *Madre América* and Álvaro Yunque's *No hay vacaciones*.

1936   President Franklin D. Roosevelt attends a Pan American conference in Buenos Aires for Latin American peace. Publication of Josefina Marpons's *44 horas semanales*.

1938   Roberto M. Ortiz, elected in September 1937, assumes the presidency.

1939   The United States reiterates the position of the Monroe Doctrine vis-à-vis the outbreak of World War II, and Argentina declares its neutrality in the conflict.

1940   Deputy Guillot commits suicide in the wake of the scandal over the irregularities of the El Palomar land sale involving the military. An ill President Ortiz delegates power to his Vice-President, Ramón S. Castillo.

1941   Argentina signs a commercial treaty with the United States. On December 16 a state of siege is declared in the country.

1942   Argentina maintains its neutrality in the wake of a meeting of Latin American chancellors in Rio de Janeiro. President

Ortiz dies less than a month after formally resigning. Publication of Luis María Albamonte's *Puerto América.*

1943   President Castillo is forced to resign under pressure from elements in the military, and General Pedro Pablo Rawson assumes the presidency; Congress is dissolved and a state of siege is declared in the wake of considerable unrest. Colonel Juan Domingo Perón is assigned to reorganize the Departamento Nacional del Trabajo. Publication of Leónidas Barletta's *La ciudad de un hombre* and Alfredo Varela's *El río oscuro.*

1944   Disastrous earthquake in San Juan and a break with the Axis powers. President Rawson hands power over to Vice-President Edelmiro J. Farrell. Perón is named Minister of War, and on July 7 he assumes the vice-presidency. The police breakup an enthusiastic public demonstration on the occasion of the liberation of Paris. On December 31 the government dissolves all political parties. Publication of José Rabinovich's *Tercera clase.*

1945   The government publishes a decree to protect national security, and Argentina declares war on Germany and Japan. State of siege is lifted and then again imposed in the face of continued social unrest; the Universities of Buenos Aires, La Plata, and El Sur are closed, and student protests are brutally repressed. Perón is imprisoned on the island of Martín García, leading to a mass demonstration in the Plaza de Mayo demanding his release; upon Perón's release, he announces his candidacy for the presidency and is married to Eva Duarte.

1946   Spruille Braden, the American ambassador, publishes the *Libro azul* denouncing Perón's candidacy; Perón wins the election. Perón's election is surrounded by a considerable exercise of executive authority in favor of the new government's ideology; a major symptomatic event is the opening of impeachment proceedings against members of the Supreme Court by the Senate. Nationalization of key foreign utilities holdings. Publication of Bernardo Kordon's *Reina del Plata* and Juan Goyanarte's *Lago argentino.*

1947   The railroads are bought from British interests. Four members of the Supreme Court are dismissed, and sufferge for women becomes law. Eva Perón's triumphant "Rainbow Tour" of

Europe to garner support for her husband's government. Publication of Bernardo Verbitsky's *En esos años*.

1949 Foreign debt payments are suspended, and a constitutional convention is convened. A new constitution allowing for presidential reelection is approved; the Peronista party is formed. In response to a minority request to investigate allegations of police brutality and torture, Congress forms a bicameral commission to investigate "anti-Argentine" activities. Publication of Carlos Ruiz Daudet's *El Pueblo*.

1950 Mass closing of newspapers by the government; approval of new law against subversive acts and the like.

1951 Closing and subsequent expropriation of the newspaper *La prensa*. Dissident army elements lead an aborted coup against Perón. Eva Perón decides not to be a candidate for Vice-President; Perón is reelected. Publication of Eva Perón's *La razón de mi vida*.

1952 Death of Eva Perón and subsequent official monumentalization of her figure.

1953 Opposition legislators are expelled from Congress.

1954 Serious conflicts between the Church and the government; a law permitting divorce takes effect.

1955 On June 16 a military uprising leads to air raids of the central part of Buenos Aires, and government-inspired thugs burn churches. The government is finally overthrown on September 16, and Perón flees into exile on a Paraguayan gunboat; General Eduardo Lonardi assumes power in the name of the Revolución Libertadora.

(A major source for information included in this chronology is Julia Elena Acuña's "Guía cronológica" in Jorge A. Paita, ed., *Argentina 1930-1960* [Buenos Aires: Sur, 1961], pp. 13-22.)

II. DEFINING THE CONTEXT

1. BERNARDO KORDON'S *REINA DEL PLATA:* SPATIALIZATION OF THE CITY IN THE NARRATIVE OF SOCIAL REALISM

The purpose of this chapter is to examine the rhetoric for the inscription of the narrative spatialization of Buenos Aires in Bernardo Kordon's narrative *Reina del Plata* (originally published in 1946 by Editorial Claridad). *Reina del Plata* is a series of interrelated fictional texts constituting a narrative that spans a period of roughly a dozen years between the Uriburu military coup of 1930 and the emerging proletariat and mass politics that Perón began to draw upon in 1943. In effect, the narrative is divided into two parts, one parenthetically titled 1930 and one 1943. Undoubtedly a time every bit as critical in the social evolution of Buenos Aires as the subsequent Peronista period that has produced so much specifically sociopolitical writing,[1] the years between 1930 and 1945 were a transition from the gilded twenties to the turbulent upheaval of the late forties and early fifties, a period marked by a violent fascist coup and by the vertiginous decline in the quality of life as a result of the depression of the thirties. It is not difficult to understand how a narrative focusing on the period of the 1930s would find especially useful the panoramic sweep of social realism, with its emphasis on the continuity of the generalized features of the communal backdrop and its manipulation

---

[1] See Andrés O. Avellaneda, "El tema del peronismo en la narrativa argentina," *Dissertation Abstracts International,* 34 (1974), 7218A; and Ernesto Goldar, *El peronismo en la literatura argentina* (Buenos Aires: Editorial Freeland, 1971).

of character and circumstance in the interests of highlighting an overall social fabric.

To say that the narrative of social realism accentuates backdrop and stresses the continuity of situational texture beyond individual destinies and particular circumstances is simply to reiterate an abiding feature of those works that strove to shift the emphasis of fiction from the representation of individual psychological cases to the documentation of the fabric of social life and from the privileged individual to the marginated outcast. However, it is not enough merely to underscore the recurring traits of a group of works. Rather, the goal of an adequate literary criticism ought to be the characterization of the pertinent strategies made use of by the writer in the attempt to provide his texts with a specific texture and sense of human "reality."

In the case of the spatialization of the city, there can be no doubt we are concerned with one of the major semiological processes of narrative actualization: the articulation of the fundamental narrative formulas in terms of a specific place or constellation of places that will contribute to the narrative's creation of meaning.[2] If, in the case of social realism, spatialization assumes greater importance than the actorilization (that is, the formulation of characters) highlighted by the romance or by the psychological novel or than the temporalization emphasized by the historical novel, it is clear that we are concerned with the dominant generative process of the narrative and must characterize it in according detail.

With respect to Kordon's nine interrelated texts (and, incidentally, each of them bears the name of one prototypic, socially-defined individual who moves through the postulated narrative space and brings together the various features that characterize it), I wish to focus on five dominant processes: 1) the irony of the title and, by extension, of the omniscient narrative voice; 2) the interplay of the exalted and the degraded; 3) a strategy of doubling whereby the narrator observes others observing the principal characters and their actions; 4) the interplay between the characters as individuals with specific personalities and the backdrop of panoramic street scenes; and 5) the juxtaposition of poetic descriptions and colloquial language.

---

[2] See "Spatialization," in A. J. Greimas, and J. Courtés, *Semiotics and Language; an Analytical Dictionary* (Bloomington: Indiana University Press, 1982), pp. 306-307.

One recalls the extensive tradition of chronicles in early Latin American literature and the subsequent flourishing of a romantic sentiment (typified so well by the lyrics of the tango) that tended to eulogize in an allegorical or hypostatic fashion the geography of the continent.[3] The title of Kordon's narrative evokes such a tradition through the use of the trope — the cliché — that translates the megapolis of Buenos Aires into a regal metaphor reinforced by the coincidence of the metaphoric name for the vast estuary on whose banks it is situated. Such tropes bear little resemblance to sociopolitical realities (the name, Río de la Plata, must certainly itself be either an allusion to the appearance of the river or to the hope that it would be an avenue of access to mineral wealth: in either case, it is one of the most inappropriate designations in the atlas), and it is the abiding irony of this fact that Kordon's title evokes.

Superimposed on a map of some of the most teeming districts of the city (Villa Crespo and Paternal stand out) the cover title announces a specifically ideological representation of the city — the space of dense human cohabitation transformed into an exalted image that will transcend the gritty facts of urban existence — that the narrative will necessarily belie in its treatment of concrete circumstances.[4] Although the trope may be maintained as a topos of the cultural tradition of the city, evoked in poetry and song and in other derived forms of cultural expression, the narrative quickly establishes the specific irony with which it is to be understood and the concrete image of the city that will serve as the backdrop of the stories to be told:

> Ya es visible el brumoso colmenar erizado de las chimeneas del Sud, el fin de cemento de la llanura argentina. La pampa muere en su caldo, en las cenagosas aguas del Plata. Pero en el mismo filo de la llanura los hombres del mundo han levantado la ciudad que la domina. "Buenos Aires, la Reina del Plata", cantaban entonces, lentos y sin gracia, los gangosos bandoneones. Y así era nomás. (p. 10)

---

[3] Bernardo de Balbuena's poem *La grandeza mexicana* (1604) comes immediately to mind as one major example of this tradition.

[4] I refer to the cover of the second edition (Buenos Aires: Editorial Jorge Álvarez, 1966). All quotes are from this edition.

Kordon's book is the story of a group of a half-dozen young men in 1930 who attempt to make a place for themselves in the vast city. Some of them are cast adrift by circumstances beyond their control as orphans or as provincials lost in the capital. Others are from middle-class families who have chosen to cast themselves adrift by renouncing what they consider to be the claustrophobic security of the family nest and by undertaking the adventure of "making it on their own." Thus, the group is of less interest as individuals with unique traits of human personality than as a range of social types that serve as indexes for particular qualities of the social fabric of Buenos Aires that Kordon wishes to characterize during the period spanning 1930-1943.

The Buenos Aires of *Reina del Plata* is, of course, the city during the turbulent period that began with the first effects of the stock market crash and with the unchecked dissolution of the second Yrigoyen government, and it is highlighted by all of the social and economic problems attendant upon the struggle for daily existence during this first of many inauspicious periods of life in modern Buenos Aires. Kordon's basic approach to the representation of the harsh realities of urban existence is by engaging his narrative in an interplay between exalted ideals of human commerce and institutions and the degraded circumstances of life out on the streets, on the level of the individuals who must struggle against all of the obstacles thrown up by an alternately monstruous and indifferent social setting.[5]

This conflict which arises from the degradation of human reality is underscored by allusions both to the political and to the economic facts of the period. For example, the description of the initially positive image of the construction of the second subway line (under

---

[5] These features of Kordon's novel are indicative of his work as a whole. See the entry by Francisco Herrera in Pedro Orgambide, and Roberto Yahni, eds., *Enciclopedia de la literatura argentina* (Buenos Aires: Editorial Sudamericana, 1970), pp. 349-350. Also of interest are Jorge Lafforgue, "Kordon, vagabundo porteño," *Davar*, No. 119 (1968), 142-146; and Jorge B. Rivera, "Estudio preliminar," in Bernardo Kordon, "*El misterioso cocinero volador*" y *otros relatos* (Buenos Aires: Centro Editor de América Latina, 1982), pp. i-x. Rivera observes, with reference to *Reina*, that "Tal vez sus muchachos que 'salen al mundo' [...] tengan algo que ver con toda una línea de relatos formativos como los que escribieron Gorki, Istrati, Hamsun, etc." (pp. iii-iv). Kordon was born in Buenos Aires in 1915, and his writings date from the early forties.

Avenida Corrientes) — one of the many signs of the much vaunted
material progress of the city — and the euphoria surrounding the
triumphal march of the army in the process of taking over the government is cut short by the detailed representation of the street
violence that broke out during the military coup and of which common citizens were victims:

> De improviso la multitud que avanzaba tuvo una sacu-
> dida de sorpresa y fue como el movimiento de una culebra
> que llenase toda la Avenida Callao. Sonaron disparos hacia
> el lado del Congreso y la incertidumbre mordió al escucharse
> nítida y brevemente una ametralladora, como una laboriosa
> máquina de coser. Nadie vio nada, pero la columna se de-
> tuvo y todo el público echó a correr presa del pánico, es-
> capando por Corrientes abajo. Al lado de Aguilera un
> hombre grueso tropezó con un tablón y se fue de narices
> al suelo. Cayó como una bolsa de harina, y ahí quedó, como
> un bulto sin vida. Aguilera lo creyó volteado por una bala,
> pero pasado el susto, el hombre se incorporó. Sonaron más
> disparos. No podían localizarse y eran iguales que en el Tiro
> Federal, estampido y después algo de chirrido. Se imaginó
> al escuadrón de policía montada corriendo detrás de ellos,
> disparándolos sus carabinas. (pp. 16-17)

Economic circumstances, on the other hand, are characterized by
the juxtaposition between the relative comfort of the children of
small businessmen and the harsh circumstances of children who spend
their waking hours hawking cheap wares in the street and who return
to sleep alone in dank and smelly tenement dwellings:

> Alejandro pensaba en sí mismo. Terminaba de cenar, y
> en su casa le esperaba su cuarto arreglado, con un velador,
> un armario con libros de estudio y un ropero con ropa limpia.
> Sus padres dormían en el dormitorio inmediato, su hermana
> en el otro. Pero para él la vida era sólo una cosa: esperar
> algo. No sabía definir bien qué cosa. ¿Cómo sería la vida
> de Mario, sin familiares, defendiéndose en la forma que
> podía? Claro que peor, pero era diferente a la suya, y por
> este mismo hecho no la consideraba del todo mala.
> —¿Por qué te dio por vender cordones? —le preguntó
> repentinamente.
> —Hace tiempo que trabajo en esto. Pero no había
> dicho nada. [...] No tengo permiso para vender. [...] Sola-

mente cuando no vendo me da rabia y soy capaz de pelearme
con todo el mundo, es cuando me siento un bicho acorra-
lado. (pp. 34-35)

Kordon's narrative strategy is to establish an inventory of references to idealized images logically subsumed within the scope of the
metaphor of the Reina del Plata: the economic growth of the city;
the monumentalized social and political myths of its generosity and
splendor; the promise extended to immigrant, provincial, and native
son to "hacer la América" thanks to the unlimited opportunities it
has to offer; the sense of adventure the young men place their
confidence in as they undertake to come of age on their own. This
inventory of commonplaces is subjected to a repeated process of
juxtaposition with the realities of existence in the city, and the details
of frustrated ambitions, mean human relations, appalling social and
economic conditions, and the numbing onslaught of the multitudes
of city dwellers all serve to provide the degraded counterimage to
the inventory of idealized qualities.

These counterimages extend from very pointed allusions to political circumstances and economic realities to more abstract and symbolic representations of an overriding sense of the disruption of the
ideal. In the following quote, the abandoned train engine becomes
the symbolic dinosaur of an enthusiasm of industrialization incapable
of assimilating it:

> Un día encontraron una [locomotora americana], abando-
> nada en una vía muerta del Puerto. Era una gigantesca má-
> quina de carga de tipo 4-8-2, comprada por el Estado, pero
> que había resultado excesivamente pesada. Durante varias
> semanas los muchachos iban a visitarla diariamente. Subían
> por la escalerilla hasta arriba del ténder, enorme como un
> vagón. Recorrían el pasadizo que atravesaba el largo de la
> caldera y trepaban hasta la caseta de mando, grande como
> una habitación. Desde el puesto del maquinista se divisaba
> los dos senos del doble domo, la chimenea, la curva de la
> ancha caldera, y muy adelante, muy lejos y pequeño, dos
> fragmentos de hierro oxidado cubiertos de pasto —la línea
> muerta—. ¡Quién pudiese dominar todo ese acero y dejarlo
> resbalar por los brillantes rieles de los que no conocían
> —ni podían suponerlos— el fin! (p. 93)

In the closing pages of the novel, two of the characters are coming to terms with themselves and with their ambitions, and the intense hustle and bustle of the streets serves to disrupt their newfound camaraderie:

> Marchaban contra la corriente humana, oleadas con botines y frágiles zapatitos sin talones y sin puntas, oleadas con casimires y con escotes, que rompían en cada bocacalle y caían en las bocas de entrada de los trenes subterráneos.
> Fiacini callóse nuevamente. Repentinamente le causó fastidio tener que conversar entre la marejada que soltaba[n] las oficinas. (p. 145)

Kordon does not dwell on the details of human misery so characteristic of the writings of the naturalists and of subsequent authors concerned to denounce specific social ills (see, for example, the section of this study devoted to Elías Castelnuovo's reform-school narrative, *Larvas*). Rather, the strategy I have described is, to a certain extent, more "psychological" in that, although the characters are not finely drawn human personalities, their individual consciousness serves to refract the clash between idealized cliché and degraded circumstance that is of fundamental importance for Kordon's narrative.

The process of refraction is enhanced by the concomitant procedure for doubling the activity of observation. If the principal thrust of the fiction is the narrative observation of a group of young men facing the inhospitable city, Kordon underscores this circumstance by portraying anonymous adults in the act of observing the former for us; this doubled observation becomes in turn a corollary of the sense of intense scrutiny of human destiny in the anonymous metropolis that characterizes the fabric of *Reina del Plata*. This refraction reinforces at the same time the narrative irony of the fiction to the extent that it further confirms the disjunction between the ideals that these young men are pursuing of independence and success and the sense of degradation and failure the older people who observe them already feel and which Kordon's work only ends up echoing.

Thus, when the boys gather in the miserable *conventillo* room to discuss the decision taken by one of them to run away from home in order to make his own way in life, they are coldly and inhospitably observed by older residents of the tenement:

> Allí fueron [los chicos]. Por un portón de hierro en-
> traron en el inquilinato. Una vieja con cara de conejo los
> observó detenidamente con sus ojillos sagaces y espanta-
> dizos. Con la cabeza baja se mantenía en guardia de todo
> lo que pudiesen hacer esos muchachos que desconocía. Pare-
> cía que los olfatease, desconfiada de la juventud.
>   En el patio de ladrillos había gente sentada en banquitos
> y sillas de paja. Piezas con cerradas cortinas de mimbres.
> Una muchacha dio vuelta la cabeza, contrariada de verse
> sorprendida en una miserable cocinita hecha de tres ma-
> deros apolillados. Un albañil italiano, desnudos los redondos
> y peludos brazos, descansaba fumando. Siguió con la vista
> a los tres muchachos, que subieron una escalera de madera,
> de astillados peldaños. [...]
>   —¡Salud, muchachos! (p. 37)

The euphoric greeting extended to his comrades by the runaway con-
trasts sharply with the implacable, silent scrutiny of the older people.

One of the boys entertains the dream of becoming a Hollywood
movie star, a fanciful flight from harsh realities into the magical
never-never-land of early cinematic fluff that Manuel Puig brilliantly
explored in *La traición de Rita Hayworth* (1968). Kordon's character
explains a sudden rage in which he beats up his girlfriend in public
as the spontaneous opportunity to "act" out a part before the stupi-
fied but morbidly curious gaze of the onlookers:

> —[...] El día que le pegué el susto a Zulema, ¿crees
> que yo estaba dopado? Ni siquiera había tomado una copa.
> Vos no comprendés: después de darle el golpe me senté en
> el Politeama, la gente me miraba y yo tuve la sensación de
> estar delante de las cámaras, sin preocuparme de que me
> señalasen con el dedo. Muy cerca mío comentaban lo ocu-
> rrido. Uno habló de llamar al vigilante y me trataba de
> cafishio. Y yo estaba muy tranquilo, encendí un cigarrillo,
> llamé al mozo y le pedí café. Todo el mundo me miraba.
> ¿Vos creés que me importaba algo? ¿Te das cuenta con
> qué clase podría trabajar en el cine [...] Me hubieses visto
> ese día: me miraban todos, y yo como si tal cosa... (p. 119)

What the observers of the scene the man recalls witness is both
a sordid realization of Fiacini's dream of becoming a movie star and
an outburst of rebellion against a stultifying existence that offers no
chance for the realization of dreams, realistic or otherwise. Although
the bystanders of this and other scenes are unable either to know

the motivations at issue or to analyze them with any degree of profundity — the omniscient narrator, of course, serves to guide the reader in this process — Kordon's strategy functions to project the conduct of his characters into the arena of the congested life of the big city where an individual cannot help but be both a voyeur of the actions of others and the object in turn of their impersonal observation.

Not all of the doubled observers are adults. In one instance, one of the characters who has been picked up by a truck driver over-hears the sordid life story of the woman whom the driver has also invited along; Julián and the woman go off together, and his act of eavesdropping defines his own particular human needs (p. 111). In another passage, one of the characters tells of having been spied upon by a little girl in the park while necking with his girlfriend. The reaction of the precocious voyeur is eloquent testimony to the sense of anger of individuals in sordid life situations and to the way in which they assume repressive and censorious postures toward the behavior of others:

> —[...] Una vez, en una plaza conversaba con una amiga. Una chica de unos nueve años, que cuidaba a un hermanito menor, pasó varias veces delante de nosotros. Nos miró de un modo especial. Muchas veces he visto mirar así pero nunca en una chica de nueve años, y eso no pudo dejar de llamarme la atención. Era una mezcla de precavido interés, de malicia y odio. Esperaba o suponía, seguramente, una escena de amor, a la que probablemente estaba acostumbrada de presenciar en el parque. A la cuarta vez que pasó, ya sin esperar más, exclamó con gesto de desprecio: " ¡Qué inmundo! " Muy posiblemente esa mocosa no supiese lo que era el amor, pero ya tenía el concepto de que se trataba de algo "inmundo". (pp. 126-127)

Although Kordon's narrative scrutiny is neither impersonal nor hostile — I have characterized it as fundamentally ironic in its skeptical stance toward the illusions of the young men — the use of other observers confirms the basic textual process of seeing the behavior of a group of representative types within the context of the city and its environs.

As a consequence of the foregoing feature of *Reina del Plata*, on a strictly thematic level, the narrative engages in an interplay between the characters as individuals with their personal, albeit prototypic, concerns and their movement against the panoramic backdrop of the city, whose impersonality, hostility, and sheer enormity is emphasized as an ironic counterpoint to their struggle both for daily survival and for personal fulfillment as human beings. Kordon's narrative is a particularly effective example of the attempt to capture this interplay at a time when the development of the city was clearly such that it could no longer be rendered, if one wished to sustain any degree of artistic honesty and integrity, in the romantic terms of, say, the tango and the tropes of "Mi Buenos Aires querido" and the like. It is for this reason that the counterpoint between individual and urban context in Kordon's work enjoys an especially foregrounded importance:

> Mario recordó que tenía que comer y sintió hambre. Se volvió hacia la Avenida de Mayo.
> En el restaurante económico "Monopol Bar" le saludaron olores de guisos en ollas cuarteleras y chamusquinas de una extensa parrilla. Un mundo de abúlicos empleadillos y adustos ganapanes, de vendedores de diarios y lustrabotas, de cuidadores de autos y bailarines de academias de baile con chillones uniformes de raso; un mundo variadísimo y completo, desde el lechuguino desplatado hasta el cargador con su arrollada soga al hombro, llamaban a gritos a los mozos que servían, o transportaban ellos mismos sus platos y sus pequeñas botellas de áspero vino tinto y sus chopes, y sin quitarse el sombrero devoraban en las pequeñas y grasientas mesas de mármol. (p. 120)

The final discursive strategy to which I wish to call attention in Kordon's novel of interrelated fragments is that of the interplay between a highly poetically imagistic description of the city and the insistently colloquial register of the various characters. Kordon's descriptions of the city are hardly romantic idealizations, as has already been noted. Yet, there is no question that his literary language reflects the assimilation of the markedly metaphoric style of the immediately preceding literary generation. The latter tended either to idealize (cf. Jorge Luis Borges's El fervor de Buenos Aires [1923]) or to poeticize the sordid (some of the early novels of the Boedo writers). Kordon engages in neither of these two écritures, choosing, rather, to use a form of imagistic expression — and only then on occasion and for relatively brief stretches of prose — to enhance the reader's sense of the growth and the imposing omnipresence of the city for his characters:

> La ciudad de cemento crecía y se levantaba como una garza blanca. Y todo ese laberinto de moles de piedras reía al sol de la aventura, al sol de infinitas posibilidades de vida. Entonces Fiacini aceptaba su puesto en la vida como un elemento flotante y a la deriva. No le interesaba la independencia por ella misma, sino como la forma de quedar a merced de los acontecimientos que acechaban en la ciudad. (p. 63)
> Las puertas que inician la ciudad son tantas como las puntas de la más complicada rosa de los vientos. Agua, asfalto y rieles de tres trochas de una docena de ferrocarriles llevan al corazón de luz y piedra. Se llega bajo nivel y sobre los terraplenes, después de mucho buscarla sobre dilatados horizontes de llanura. Buenos Aires, por el laberinto perfumado de delta, por los patriarcales ríos densos que bajan del trópico. Buenos Aires por el asfalto y por sus [sic] espantosa maraña de rieles — su cabellera de plata. (p. 100)

This is a form of expression that undoubtedly has its roots in the writing developed by the vanguard poets for achieving both a hypostasis and a pathetic fallacy for the city that hithertofore had been evoked in the sentimental terms of local color motifs and quaint characteristics. Just as there is nothing quaint or sentimental about the poetic representations of Borges, Eduardo and Raúl González Tuñón, or Nicolás Olivari, Kordon's descriptions are an integral part of his creation of the sense of a physical space for the movement of a human multitude that interacts in an immediate fashion with this space.

By contrast and in eloquent counterpoint to these evocations, the integers of this multitude express themselves in the most direct, flat, and unmetaphoric form possible. Without achieving the gritty colloquial texture of the characters of an earlier writer like Roberto Arlt or of a later novelist like Enrique Medina (a writer who represents the apotheosis of contemporary degraded Buenos Aires), the speech of Kordon's characters typifies their almost anonymous integration in the all-consuming metropolis:

> —Sí, estoy solo. Hace cosa de un año me fui de casa. Y no, no fue para ser algo sino para no ser nada y vivir. ¿No le parece que es lo principal? En esta valijita no llevo

ropa de fútbol, ni de box, ni de nada parecido. ¿Sabe lo qué
[sic] hay? Pomadas, peines, cordones. Me lo facilitó un
amigo. Pero no tengo ganas de ofrecer a la gente. ¿Cómo
voy a andar por la calle vendiendo estas porquerías? ¿Para
eso me fui de casa, dejé todo? (pp. 64-65)

The sense of abandon, of rootlessness, of absolute solitude reflected in this declaration confirms Kordon's vision of the loss of identity
in Buenos Aires of the period his novel portrays.

Reina del Plata, like many of the works of the writers of the
1930s and 1940s in Argentina, has not enjoyed wide acclaim, although the fact that it was reprinted twenty years after its original
publication and has been reprinted again recently is indicative of its
representative merit. This merit lies in the competence with which
Kordon undertakes to provide a sense of the evolving city as the
arena for the playing out of a symptomatic array of human ambitions
among a social class that experienced considerable growth in Buenos
Aires during the period in question. Kordon's novel is based essentially on pathetic fallacy, a circumstance that clearly makes its diver-
gence from romanticized versions of the metropolis like the classical
Gardelian tango.

Rather than conceiving of the city as an anthropomorphized
mirror of the suffering of unique, foregrounded individuals, *Reina
del Plata* operates on the principle that the human types it surveys
in kaleidoscopic fashion are accurate indexes of inherent qualities of
the city as an organic if monstrous presence. It is in this sense that
Kordon's novel is such a faithful example of the varieties of social
realism in Argentina and of the attempt of that movement to reassess
the bases of rational life.

2. LEÓNIDAS BARLETTA'S *LA CIUDAD DE UN HOMBRE*: ADAM'S WORLD

> Mario escuchaba y callaba. Comprendía que ahora el miedo y no otra cosa, movía la cruel maquinaria represiva. (p. 178)

> —Hace falta equivocarse, y sufrir —dijo él [i.e., Mario]—. Hay que ir al encuentro de la desgracia. Ya tengo treinta y un años. Y no he hecho más que rodar en esta ciudad que es otro de mis amores. Aquí he vivido y sufrido y en muchas esquinas he ido dejando un poco de mi alma. Y yo siento que Buenos Aires, es un poco como yo mismo, impulsivo, franco, desordenado, triste, generoso, soñador, qué se [*sic*] yo... Hay gente que le gusta este barrio o aquél... Yo los entiendo a todos... Y cada día voy comprendiendo más el alma de los que viven y sufren, aquí, con nosotros... (pp. 292-293) [1]

Although usually identified with the Boedo group of writers — those authors and intellectuals who during the vanguard period of the 1920s identified with the cause of Argentina's large and restless proletariat — Leónidas Barletta (1902-1975) continued to exercise considerable influence during the period of social realism that is of interest to this study. [2] The author of an impressive body of creative

---

[1] Leónidas Barletta, *La ciudad de un hombre; novela* (Buenos Aires: Santiago Rueda-Editor, 1943).

[2] There is relatively scant criticism on Barletta. See the entry by Pedro Orgambide in his and Roberto Yahni's *Enciclopedia de la literatura argentina* (Buenos Aires: Editorial Sudamericana, 1970), pp. 77-79; José Pedroni, "Noticia y estimación de Leónidas Barletta," *Bibliograma*, No. 40 (1968), 5-9; and Noé Jitrik, "Los comunistas (Manauta, Barletta, Yunque, Varela)," *Contorno*,

literature, Barletta nevertheless was perhaps the most influential for having founded the Teatro del Pueblo in 1930, one of the first of the major Teatro Independiente groups over a twenty-five year period beginning approximately in that year.[3] Barletta convinced Roberto Arlt, then attracting much attention with the publication of his key novel *Los siete locos* (1929), to write for the Teatro del Pueblo. The body of Expressionistic, Pirandellian works Arlt wrote and produced thanks to Barletta's instigation during the intense ten-year period before his untimely death in 1942 have come to be considered pivotal texts in the development of the Argentine theater of the period.[4]

Barletta's Teatro del Pueblo, in addition to its broader program of contributing to the development of a well-defined theatrical consciousness among the Argentine public of all social levels, was especially committed to the goals of proletarian art, and the enterprise engaged in a number of strategies and activities designed to respond to the need for proletarian culture: popular prices; theater in the streets, plazas, and workplaces; and discussion sessions after the final curtain between actors and audience over the nature of the work just presented.[5] Although these efforts probably did not lead to much art *by* the proletariat (one of the goals of similar movements in the United States), it did provide the working class with access to a type of professional theater of considerable originality and social commitment.

In part because of his many personal involvements with the causes of social realism and proletarian literature and undoubtedly to a large degree as the result of the sustained public activity of

---

Nos. 5-6 (1955), 49. The most complete overview of Barletta's work remains Juan Pinto's "Leónidas Barletta, novelista de su tiempo," in his *Literatura argentina del siglo XX; 1.ª serie* (Buenos Aires: Ediciones Argentina "S.I.A.", 1943), pp. 86-114. Unfortunately, the novel studied in this essay had not been published by the date of Pinto's commentary.

[3] See the comments on the Teatro del Pueblo in Luis Ordaz, *El teatro en el Río de la Plata, desde sus orígenes hasta nuestros días;* 2.ª ed. corr. y aum. (Buenos Aires: Ediciones Leviatán, 1957), pp. 207-209.

[4] I examine the contributions of Arlt in "Roberto Arlt," in *Critical Survey of World Drama* (Englewood Cliffs, N.J.: Salem Press, forthcoming), and in my *The Argentine Teatro Independiente* (York, S.C.: Spanish Literature Publications, forthcoming).

[5] Luis Ordaz provides this information on the Teatro del Pueblo in his "Teatro: desde la generación intermedia a la actualidad," in *Capítulo: la historia de la literatura argentina* (Buenos Aires: Centro Editor de América Latina, 1967-68), No. 52, pp. 1233-37.

projects like the Teatro del Pueblo, Barletta's writing demonstrates a sustained involvement in the artistic and political issues of the period without his ever actually authoring a text that could be called denunciatory in the sense of the work of Alfredo Varela or Elías Castelnuovo or revolutionary in the sense of Álvaro Yunque.

Like Bernardo Kordon, Barletta saw his primary interest as lying with the representation of the thoughts, feelings, moods, and values of the urban lumpen and with chronicling the events and movements of the period that impinged on and formed the consciousness of his characters. And like Eduardo Mallea, the Argentine writer of the period who, justly or unjustly, deservedly or thanks to the backing he received from various Establishment fora, achieved the greatest international prominence, writers like Barletta and Yunque, and Arlt in the preceding decade, were concerned to portray the sense of loss and rootlessness of the Argentine citizen. Mallea, of course, focused on the existential anguish of upper-middle class and aristocratic in-dividuals, while the latter concerned themselves with working-class men and (on a few occasions) women, for whom the sense of general despair and aimlessness is made all the more accute for the economic deprivations they must also experience. One might note that, for all his putative elitism, Mallea was much less sexually biased than the social realists: where the bulk of their characters are men, some of Mallea's most memorable *argentinos invisibles* are women, like Ágata Cruz of *Todo verdor perecerá* (1941).

Barletta's *La ciudad de un hombre* (1948) is particularly repre-sentative of this form of social realist writing. The backdrop of the novel is the panorama of historical events stretching from the birth of the protagonist, Mario, before World War I, to a time approx-imately five years after the Uriburu fascist coup of 1930. Mario witnesses Argentina's minimal involvement in the war (he sells his beloved horse to a "man in a boy scout uniform" who is buying animals to be shipped to the European battlefields), the chaotic period of the Yrigoyen presidency and the various strikes and manifestations of workers' demands during the period, the turmoil of the 1930 takeover, and the transformations that affect the city during the early 1930s as part of the strengthening of Argentine and interna-tional capital in the city. Mario is both an observing eye who bears testimony to the social and political changes occurring around him, changes that he gauges in terms of his own individual problems and preoccupations, but he is also an Adamic figure. Mario is a figure of Adam to the extent that his personal suffering is the result of the socioeconomic forces at work during the period as well as a consequence of the particular existential anguish of the human consciousness, and it is clear that Barletta's novel is the *Bildungsroman* of one exceptionally representative consciousness of Buenos Aires as an archetypic City of Man.

Yet, it is necessary to qualify the use of the term *Bildungsroman,* since there is a fundamental difference between such a mode in the fiction of traditional realism and in social realism. In the case of the former, what is essentially at issue is the evolution of the consciousness, the personality, of main characters in tandem with their integration or lack of it in the prevailing bourgeois society. One pattern involves the process of assimilation between the hero and established bourgeois order, no matter how the latter may be critically presented (e.g., so many of Dickens's heroes). However, Georg Lukács has shown in his famous study on masterpieces of European realism,[6] such novels quite frequently meant the representation of the alienation of the individual from society — e.g., Flaubert's *Madame Bovary* or Tolstoi's *Anna Karenina*. It is, of course, Lukács examination of a prevalent form of fiction that traces the growing disjunction between the individual, portrayed in terms of an evolving consciousness, and the established social order that establishes a point of reference for those novels of social realism concerned with the characters' states of consciousness and not just their social behavior.

The novel alternates in relentless fashion the manifestations of Mario's sense of personal loss and the projections of his feeling of an almost euphoric hope in the face of individual and collective physical and emotional deprivations. Mario is witness to an entire range of depressing and degrading situations. The initial loss of his mother and the breakup of the home by a father who farms his three sons out to various relatives rather than assume parental responsibility for them is complemented by the deficient care received by the children at the hands of an array of indifferent and misguided relatives. During one idyllic period, Mario and one of his brothers are kept by an uncle and his common-law wife, and Mario experiences

---

[6] *Studies in European Realism* (New York: Grosset & Dunlap, 1964).

the pleasures of rural life under the tutelage of the uncle, who is clearly obsessed with the gaucho myths of *Don Segundo Sombra* (Ricardo Güiraldes's 1926 pastoral novel). However, the uncle disappears one day, apparently driven by guilt to return to his legal family, and once again Mario witnesses the dissolution of a nurturing family unit. Now old enough to defend himself on his own in the streets, Mario moves in the Arltian world of the large and hostile city, experiencing the horrors of a seedy hotel for transients and becoming familiar with such typical institutions as the brothel, the hospital, the army, and an assortment of cabarets.

Unlike Arlt, however, Barletta is convinced that the individual can survive with hope in his own future, and in this sense Barletta shares the unswerving optimism of the proletariat movement that exercised no persuasive hold of the intensely pessimistic author of *Los siete locos*. Thus, as Mario moves through the prototypic settings I have enumerated, his sense of despair in the face of the humiliation of the individual they personify is ameliorated by an equally profound involvement with examples of the great brotherhood of mankind as it manifests itself in the sprawling city. Thus, he is taken in by a series of humble workmen and street vendors, becomes involved in the Communist Party and its public activities, and in the end is virtually adopted as a junior partner by a Jewish dry goods merchant who entrusts him with the responsibility of dealing with the blackmarketeers from whom the merchant obtains his silk goods (this detail is an important aspect on the nature of doing business in Argentina during the so-called Infamous Decade of the 1930s). Although "positive" examples of Mario's range of personal experiences are repeatedly marked by the same sign of loss that characterized the breakup of his parents' home, a sign of Edenic exile that underscores the protagonist's qualities as an Adamic figure, it is precisely his need to move from one tenuous refuge to another that allows both the panoramic sweep of the novel and the development of his personal consciousness as a prototypic witness to social change.

As a consequence, *La ciudad de un hombre* is essentially mosaic in nature, and the narrative consists of brief segments that rarely exceed one or two pages. The role of the narrator is both to situate Mario in a succession of circumstances and to characterize directly and indirectly his emerging consciousness as to the nature of human experience in a city like Buenos Aires during specific historical moments. Thus, on numerous occasions the narrator portrays the texture of city life with direct references to the formation of Mario's self-image as an individual and a member of a concrete social reality:

> Todo ese mundo de gente que ocupaba la ciudad para siempre o de paso, venían a su encuentro: los vigilantes de cada esquina, los cocheros, los carteros con su gran bolsa de cuero, y los animales de la ciudad, los canarios de las fondas que tomaban el sol de la vereda, junto con las desteñidas plantas que adornaban el comedor; los gatos ondulantes y los perros que correteaban por las calles hasta que los chicos los espantaban a pedradas para que no los enlazase el perrero.
>
> Y poco a poco fue sintiendo la ciudad, con sus estaciones de ferrocarril, sus circos, sus bodegones, sus mercados, sus cementerios.
>
> El andar y su angustia lo hicieron sabio. Pensaba. Siempre iba rumiando cosas. (p. 111)
>
> Es muy difícil decir cómo se siente una ciudad; pero está toda ella en el corazón, y cuando se dice plaza se sabe que esta palabra es insignificante y no corresponde a cada una de las plazas de Buenos Aires y mucho menos a la montañita de la plaza Vicente López, al pie de la que había un guayabo que encendía la imaginación de los chicos; ni la alfombra amarilla que tendían los paraísos de la plaza Garay; ni la sombra azulada de los jacarandás de la Plaza de Mayo, con la Casa Rosada, requemada por el sol de la tarde. La memoria de la gran ciudad guarda con idéntico cuidado un trozo de vereda y un ángulo de techumbre. [...]
>
> Y él, Mario, se estaba allí, en la esquina, con las manos en el bolsillo, silbando, lo que acentuaba su soledad, porque nadie silba para otro. El silbido obliga a poner cara seria y si la mirada del otro lo hace sonreír el silbido se desinfla. El que silba hace música para oírse, para sí mismo y a veces el silbido es la voz disimulada, que inicia un sollozo. (pp. 260-261)

The literature of all metropolitan writers is characteristically marked by a sense of the city and of its qualities as a paradigm of human society in all of its complexity. The works of Buenos Aires authors are no different in this regard.[7] Barletta's novel, with its

---

[7] One of the standard photobooks on Buenos Aires contains texts by major authors on the city: *Buenos Aires, mi ciudad* (Buenos Aires: Editorial Universitaria de Buenos Aires, 1963).

sense of the humiliation of the individual in the monstrous and protean city continues the vision of his close associate Roberto Arlt and foreshadows, as one of a variegated inventory of texts, the unrelentingly negative portrait of the city in contemporary novels that I have called the "demythification" of Buenos Aires.[8] But what makes *La ciudad de un hombre* pertinent to the present study is not only the proletarian odyssey of Mario, for his personal story is that of the son of a solidly middle-class family who comes to maturity in the settings of the worker-class reality into which he "falls" by accident, but the fact that Barletta's protagonist through it all bespeaks the quintessential optimism of human survival. Like the closing words of William Faulkner's 1929 *The Sound and the Fury,* with reference to the blacks, "They endured," the closing pages of Barletta's novel show Mario emerging from one of the bitterest of his personal trials to face life with renewed hope: "Una ciudad es como una trinchera de la civilización. Se emocionó pensando que a Buenos Aires, a la que tanto quería, el destino podría haberle reservado la gran misión" (p. 324).

---

[8] David William Foster, "The Demythification of Buenos Aires in Selected Argentine Novels of the Seventies," *Chasqui,* 10, 1 (1980), 3-25.

3. DEFINING STRATEGIES IN RAÚL SCALABRINI ORTIZ'S *EL HOMBRE QUE ESTÁ SOLO Y ESPERA*

> Sin aspavientos, agazapado en la mansa llaneza de su naturalidad emotiva, el hombre porteño revalora al mundo. Aprehendiendo y mensurando el mundo en sí mismo, dilucidando sus afirmaciones en el contraste sin sospecha de sus propios sentimientos, el hombre porteño aventa las teorizaciones arqueológicas, poda la ampulosidad de los conceptos, humilla la arrogancia de los contextos legalistas y manumite al hombre de la artificiosa hojarasca literaria que le recubría y le suplantaba en el dictamen de los hombres. (p. 111) [1]

Although the major prose texts of social realism in Argentina are fictional, there are two major book-length essays that impinge upon the interests of the novelists of the period because of the contributions to the definition of a proletarian or countercultural image of Argentine society. I have examined elsewhere in detail the rhetorical strategies of Ezequiel Martínez Estrada's monumental *Radiografía de la pampa* (1933). [2] *Radiografía* is a work that proposes the deconstruction of a vast network of official myths concerning Argentine social and cultural history, positing in their place precisely Martínez Estrada's pessimistic, Spenglerian vision of the decline of Argentine national identity. While this essay, which runs around four

---

[1] Raúl Scalabrini Ortiz, *El hombre que está solo y espera;* 11.ª ed. (Buenos Aires: Plus Ultra, 1971).

[2] David William Foster, "*Radiografía de la pampa,* de Martínez Estrada, como una lectura desconstructivista de la Argentina," in his *Para una lectura semiótica del ensayo latinoamericano: textos representativos* (Madrid: José Porrúa Turanzas, 1983), pp. 99-116.

hundred pages, is hardly Marxist, communist, or socialist in its interpretations (Martínez Estrada will, however, embrace the cause of the Cuban revolution thirty years later, reside for a period in Cuba, and write an important analysis of José Martí),[3] it is nevertheless part of the project of the 1930s, during the height of the fascist *década infame,* to write against the grain of prevailing and self-serving institutionalized versions of Argentina.

Raúl Scalabrini Ortiz (1898-1959) had published his far briefer essay *El hombre que está solo y espera* in 1931. The numerous reprintings and reeditions it has gone through in subsequent years attest to its greater popularity than Martínez Estrada's more ponderous and intellectual essay. Indeed, Scalabrini Ortiz, who was to go on to write a series of important denunciations of the exploitation of foreign capital in Argentina in the form of British ownership of the national railway system, clearly appealed to popular readers in a way that Martínez Estrada could not.[4] Moreover, their interpretations are markedly different. By contrast to the latter's oppressive pessimism, Scalabrini Ortiz paints an idealized portrait of the Argentine common man, certainly a typical undertaking during a period of proletarian concern. His Hombre de Corrientes y Esmeralda is the *typus* for the lower-middle class urban man whose roots may be among the large colonies of foreign immigrants who changed the face of Buenos Aires during the fifty-year period between 1880 and 1930, but whose values, whose sense of identity, and whose entire personality profile is intensely and profoundly Argentine.

The essay undertakes to sketch, in a style that is both pithy and poetically evocative (almost pretentiously so), the distinguishing features of this prototype to be found, symbolically, at the intersection of the two downtown streets, Corrientes and Esmeralda.[5] Al-

---

[3] *Martí revolucionario* (La Habana: Casa de las Américas, 1967); see also his *Martí; el héroe y su acción revolucionaria* (México, D.F.: Siglo XXI, 1966). Alexander Coleman examines Martínez Estrada's relationship to Martí in "Martí y Martínez: historia de una simbiosis espiritual," *Revista iberoamericana,* Nos. 92-93 (1975), 629-645.

[4] *Los ferrocarriles, factor principal de la independencia nacional* (1937), *Historia de los ferrocarriles argentinos* (1940), and *Los ferrocarriles deben ser del pueblo argentino* (1947).

[5] See the following critical material on Scalabrini and his essay: Attilo Dabini, "*El hombre que está solo y espera,*" in Pedro Orgambide, and Roberto Yahni, *Enciclopedia de literatura argentina* (Buenos Aires: Editorial Sudameri-

though Scalabrini Ortiz's portrait lacks the humorous and slapstick quality of Damon Runyon's writing, there is undoubtedly a parallel in their respective attempts to give a sense of the often anonymous and essentially overlooked man of the street and to portray the essential dignity beneath the mask that encourages rejection of them by their social "betters": their smarminess in the case of Runyon's types, their detached and sardonical privateness in the case of Scalabrini's Hombre.

My concern here, however, is not with recounting the details of Scalabrini Ortiz's interpretation of the Hombre de Corrientes y Esmeralda. His exposition is quite forthright. Although there is much to discuss with regard to his interpretation in terms of both the accuracy of his judgments fifty years ago and the pertinence of them for present-day Argentine society, the principal interest of his essay for this study concerns the rhetorical strategies employed in that exposition. Not a narrative text, *El hombre que está solo y espera* bears a direct relationship to the material dealt with in this study because of its attempt to characterize a stratum of Argentine social reality that, if it had been of any concern at all in other, earlier writers, it was only for the purposes of dismissal as either not pertinent to the representation of "real" Argentina (i.e., that defined by the mythopoeic oligarchy) or as simply a derivative of the barbarian aspects of the lower classes (that is, the repudiation of those indigenous, Creole, and immigrant strains that could not comfortably be assimilated into the dominant model).

In reality, it is not surprising that Scalabrini's essay be so characterized by poetic eloquence, hyperbole, and subjective interpretation: these are simply traces — overt, explicit textual features — that attest to the underlying imperative to portray emphatically as a paradigmatic social model a character type that was only beginning to emerge as a sort of cultural hero under the aegis of the loosely-

---

cana, 1970), pp. 209-210; Adolfo Prieto, "Consideraciones sobre 'El hombre que está solo y espera'," *Boletín de literaturas hispánicas,* No. 3 (1961), 23-40; also as "*El hombre que está solo y espera,*" in his *Estudios de literatura argentina* (Buenos Aires: Editorial Galerna, 1969), pp. 57-81; Dardo Cúneo, "La crisis argentina del '30 en Güiraldes, Scalabrini Ortiz y Lugones," *Cuadernos hispanoamericanos,* No. 140 (1965), 158-174; and Raúl Larra, "Scalabrini Ortiz, una conciencia nacional," in his *Etcétera* (Buenos Aires: Ánfora, 1982), pp. 129-136. A fragment of *Hombre* was published in English translation in *Living Age* [New York], January 1934, pp. 416-421.

defined proletarian ideologies of the 1930s. Scalabrini's Hombre may not be a proletarian in any proper sense of the word: he is portrayed as typically a minor bureaucrat or office worker. But he is legitimized as such not only because of his typically humble origins but, most importantly, because of his social anonymity and margination. José María Rosa characterizes this Hombre in the following terms in his introduction (dated 1964) to the essay:

> En *El hombre que está solo y espera,* Scalabrini analizó al argentino de la década del 30 y primeros años del 40. Es un *multígeno,* producto del entrechoque de muchas razas, pero de ninguna manera un híbrido; Adán Buenos Aires no puede ser explicado por la materia que lo forma, ni por la índole de la enseñanza recibida. Su corazón le ha permitido presentir la falsedad de aquello aprendido en la escuela o leído en los editoriales de la prensa cotidiana. Ha comprendido que esa *libertad* que le dijeron era la patria misma, servía de ganzúa para un dominio extranjero; que esa *democracia* alabada como un culto, se ejercería sin pueblo en los comicios oficiales y sin voluntad de pueblo en los comités opositores; que esa *constitución* "la más sabia del mundo", servía para los barridos y fregados de la minoría gobernante que administraba los intereses foráneos en la tranquila colonia que éramos; que esa *historia argentina* que le enseñaron presentaba como ejemplos próceres a quienes hicieron posible esa enajenación espiritual y material que lo había reducido a simple espectador, desde Corrientes y Esmeralda, del acaecer político de la Argentina. Ha sabido así que no tiene maestros ni libros; que debe hacerlo todo por sí mismo. (p. 11)

Rosa, thus, leaves no doubt as to the Hombre's definition, in the terminology of the 1960s, as a countercultural spokesman and as an individual whose basic axiological profile may be considered in terms of his categorical opposition to the dominant myths of this society.

However, Rosa's characterization, which ends with an allusion to a solitary deontic activism, should not lead us to view Scalabrini's Hombre as the proletarian leader sought by the revolutionary calls to action of the period. *El hombre que está solo y espera* may dwell appropriately on an example of social margination, but the two operative qualifiers of his title, being alone and waiting, belie the call to collective, revolutionary action that we typically associate with proletarian literature.

Indeed, the first of the rhetorical strategies I wish to focus on concerns the author's assertion that not only is his characterization a personal and subjective one and not only is he assuming the burden of representing for society a prevalent *typus* that had not previously been acknowledged to exist, but that it is likely that the object of his characterization would take exception to the author's very representation:

> Y ahora ya en la poscomunión de este oficio que nos reveló el misterio de una soledad sexual, escondámonos, lector, para espiar los juicios, las preferencias y las inclinaciones del hombre. Si él nos descubre nos fraguará un ardid: él no quiere que su intimidad se viole ni aun a precio de gloria. Él quiere permanecer solo, con su deseo ya tan confederado a otros que la ciudad entera se testifica en él. (p. 52)

> Hasta el mismo Hombre de Corrientes y Esmeralda, si leyera estos apuntes, se armaría de sospechas y pensaría: "Éste nos está cachando". Pero no nos descompongamos y abordemos el tema tranquilos. (pp. 103-104)

Scalabrini, of course, is not denying the validity of his portrait nor is he really justifying in an oblique fashion the role of the social commentator or novelist as a voyeur who "spies" upon the objects of his analysis in order better to reveal aspects of their being they would vociferously deny. Rather, Scalabrini is engaging here in a form of double hyperbole. On the first hand, his allegation that the Hombre would react sardonically to the essay's analysis is a way of underscoring the reserve and the sense of privacy of the personality being discussed. The inviolateness of this *soledad* can lead the Hombre to belie even a faithful characterization of his nature, and *El hombre que está solo y espera* can only function as a suspension of this criterion. Thus, the readers are assured that they are being given a privileged glimpse of a prevalent but self-effacing social type. The interplay between the eloquence of Scalabrini Ortiz's essay and the characteristic silent solitude of the Hombre enhances the author's claim to be providing the reader with a privileged access to a significant human nature, but it also confirms the extent to which the Hombre does not conform to the ideal of activist leader that Rosa's description might imply. [6]

---

[6] Prieto makes the point that "Scalabrini expone sus observaciones dentro de la levedad de un impresionismo sociológico puesto a la moda por Ortega"

Hyperbole is undoubtedly one of the prominent textual markers of Scalabrini's essay, and it corresponds to the insistent need to characterize emphatically a disjunctive social type, one that exists in opposition to prevailing national myths and ignored by them. The solitude and the almost aboulic detachment of the Hombre are, of course, essential and strategic exaggerations, as are the descriptions of many of the contributing elements in his origins and his place in society. Scalabrini has chosen to represent an abstract, an ideal model that is primarily defined in terms of what he is not (i.e., national myths, prevailing ideologies, outdated shibboleths), and the abundant use of hyperbole points out the alternate, distinguishing features that the essayist would have his reader accept as noteworthy and accurate:

> No menosprecia las personas, le son indiferentes. Así se explica la atonía con que la ciudad acoge a los hombres que la emocionaron con sus proezas deportivas en países extranjeros. Llegan, se les festeja con un saludito de bienvenida, se barbulle su hazaña un día y se les sume en un olvido absoluto. Al mes de cometer su hazaña, Lindberg, en Buenos Aires, hubiera sido un desconocido, un aviador osado y pobrete. (p. 61)

> En el caos inextricable de la vida porteña, la inteligencia es incapaz de soluciones. Solamente el arrojo del instinto induce probabilidades y propicia rutas. El Hombre de Corrientes y Esmeralda confía ciegamente en sus "pálpitos" de última hora. El pálpito es la brújula que no enloquece en la marejada porteña, en su frenético vaivén de cuerpo afuera. (p. 76)

In this way, the hyperbole serves to stress the Hombre's reluctance to indulge in excessive enthusiasm as part of his critical and sardonic stance toward facile pretensions or to place emphasis on the Hombre's distrust of rationalizations that deny his legitimate human intuitions in contact with the daily give-and-take of life. In all of

---

(*Estudios*, p. 71), and that the author does not really engage in profound sociopolitical analysis until he subsequently writes his treatises on the railroads: "No hay en estos libros impresionismo sociológico, abundancia de intuiciones ni interpretaciones metahistóricas. Hay un intento de explicar, con el manejo de datos concretos y de cifras aún más concretas, el usufructo de la economía nacional por intereses extranjeros y la consecuente deformación de la historia nacional. Ninguno de estos datos habían sido utilizados para la redacción de *El hombre que está solo y espera*" (p. 80).

these cases, hyperbole functions as an effective strategy for discriminating between an assumed social norm and prevalent national character and the unique *typus* that Scalabrini Ortiz proposes to identify and portray for the reader.

Another related strategy is the disjunctive rhetorical formula "no A, sino B," an especially effective device in the sense that it permits the explicit rejection of one situation or characteristic in favor of another, putatively more real or accurate one. The general scheme here is the essayist's premise that the Hombre de Corrientes y Esmeralda, as the prototypical urban man, is *not* what has been identified as the Argentine national character by prevailing shibboleths, *but* the sort of *typus* developed by *El hombre que está solo y espera*. Moreover, the author tends to embed his disjunctive enumerations in statements that are both hyperbolic and reiterative, the latter quality serving in reality as a constituent of the hyperbole:

> La primera impresión que percutió el instinto del Hombre de Corrientes y Esmeralda, *no* provino de las percepciones que cosechaban sus sentidos: *no* fue un tacto que se exacerbó, *no* fue una erectilidad de sus ojos hechizados, *no* fue una enajenación de los oídos enternecidos por la fragancia de una promesa, *no* fue, tampoco, el reconocimiento de dos destinos que hallaban en el apareamiento de sus cuerpos la expresión de una voluntad más alta. **Fue** un egoísta estremecimiento de su fantasía atenaceada por un incipiente apetito cerril, **fue** una delirante, aunque borrosa fábula, una imagen brutalmente desarraigada de la vida, y *no* una criatura real, con sus inherencias, sus virtudes, sus pecados. **Fue** una creación, *no* una conquista, la primera conquista del adolescente porteño. (pp. 57-58)

The italics and boldface that I have added to this quote underline the segments of the disjunctive formula. The italics represent the "no A" half of the characterization — those elements that might be attributed to the Hombre but which the essayist is rejecting as incorrect — and the boldface represents the "sino B" segments which are the features the text has assigned as correct and appropriate to the prototype.

Early in his essay, Scalabrini speaks of the difficulty of his enterprise, again a rhetorical ploy designed to heighten our sense of the uniqueness of his interpretation and the discrimination of his vision vis-à-vis established types. Thus, "La tarea es desalentadora"

(p. 21) and "La expedición es riesgosa" (p. 22). Hence, "Construirlo todo, todo, y he allí lo desalentador, hasta la misma realidad" (p. 23), an estimation that forgives the essayist for whatever inaccuracy as a complete construct of reality his interpretations may have. When Scalabrini cautions the reader in the following terms, we understand that he is to be given credit for not having been deterred in his pursuit of a faithful representation:

> Mas no se intente remontar el curso meandroso de los sentimientos de ese admirador efímero y desinteresado, porque el porteño despistará al impertinente que se atreve a expugnar su confianza. Se agazapará, prevenido, y desconcertará al intruso con una estimación burlesca o un ex abrupto cínico. (p. 27)

I do not mean to imply that Scalabrini Ortiz is disingenuous in his definition of the task he has undertaken or that he reveals an unweaning self-flattery for what he implies his accomplishments to have been. It is simply that this sort of framing of the nature of his project to characterize the Hombre de Corrientes y Esmeralda is an appropriate rhetorical strategy for confirming the elusive nature of his subject.

Yet, not all of Scalabrini's rhetorical strategies are based on the implications of a negative postulation. One of the most attractive features about the essay for anyone who is familiar with the colloquial Spanish of Buenos Aires is the essayist's quotation of the Hombre's expressive clichés. These clichés — and, to be sure, a similar lexical phenomenon exists in all languages — are ready-made and fossilized phrases or sentences, colloquial tropes, that are used as pathetic responses to given social situations and to describe certain personal reactions to issues and events. Scalabrini Ortiz cites these expressions in quotation marks, brandishing them as linguistic metonyms for the sociocultural point of view of his Porteño prototype:

> "¿Pa qué deslomarse si tu suerte es reventar" (p. 42, with reference to taking one's work too seriously)
>
> "[...] ¡Cómo pasa el tiempo! ¡Parece que fue ayer" (p. 50, with reference to recollecting a pleasant memory of an activity)
>
> "Che, no se quería dejar besar y la atropellé detrás del saguán" (p. 59, referring to the boastful machismo that speaks, at the very least, of women as objects of possession and rape)

"Vaya a saber cómo fue" (p. 69, as a verbal shrug of the shoulders)

"No te metás" (p. 73, to indicate, rather than just that one should mind his or her own business, that it is better not to get involved)

"Estos yonis son una luz para los pesos" (p. 89, as a sardonic encomium of other people's industriousness; *yoni* here is slang for Britisher, from "Johnny")

"Y entonces... ¿qué te crees [*sic,* for creés]?" (p. 107, a phrase used not necessarily to repudiate what the interlocutor has said, but for lack of anything better to say)

The nineteen principal fragments of *El hombre que está solo y espera* are built around approximately one hundred of these clichés or tropes (there are three additional segments, "Libreta de apuntes," Scalabrini's own sardonic devil's-dictionary definitions of several dozen key concepts; and two poetic evocations, "Connotación de fugacidades" and "Acentos de soledad"). Each of the principal segments is a descriptive noun phrase that refers to one of the aspects of the Hombre de Corrientes y Esmeralda: "El hijo de nadie," "La ciudad sin amor," "El místico sin Dios," "El patrón de sí mismo."

The rhetorical strategies that I have identified provide the essential texture for these mosaic sketches that run from five to six pages on the average. References to the essayist's privileged perspective and to the difficulty of his task (primarily in the initial segments), hyperbolic characterizations of key points and the disjunctive identification of hackneyed concepts to be repudiated in favor of accurate qualities, and (especially in the middle and final segments) an abundant use of the actual expressive commonplaces of the *typus* all serve to substantiate Scalabrini Ortiz's specific interpretation of the Porteño character:

El Hombre de Corrientes y Esmeralda es un ritmo de las vibraciones comunes, un magnetismo en que todo lo porteño se imana, una aspiración que sin pertenecer en dominio a nadie está en todos alguna vez. Lo importante es que todos sientan que hay mucho de ellos en él y presientan que en condiciones favorables pueden ser enteramente análogos. El Hombre de Corrientes y Esmeralda es un ente ubicuo: es el hombre de las muchedumbres, el croquis activo de sus líneas genéricas, algo así como la columna vertebral de sus pasiones. Es, además, el protagonista de una novela planeada por mí, que ojalá alguna vez alcance el mérito de no haber sido publicada. (pp. 33-34)

Scalabrini Ortiz never published the novel he claims to have had in mind, and *El hombre que está solo y espera* rightly remains his most lasting contribution to Argentine literature and a truly representative piece of writing of the thirties in that country.

4. LUIS MARÍA ALBAMONTE'S *PUERTO AMÉRICA*: THE IMMIGRANT EXPERIENCE

> A veces le parecía que era un barco. El barco
> en el cual había viajado. Con las mismas angustias,
> las mismas esperanzas, idénticas miserias. Un barco
> sucio, miserable. En él no había nadie que
> le diese alegría. Nada. [...] Era una ansiedad como
> una sofocación. Permanente. (p. 92) [1]

One supposes that any novel with a happy ending for the trial of the lone individual is ipso facto precluded from serious consideration as an example of social realism. The urgent imperative to represent a specific demythificational, denunciatory, and militant attitude toward the crucial elements of Argentine social experience and the rhetorical need to embody this attitude in a narrative trajectory that bespoke either a revolutionary promise or a crushing defeat of legitimate human aspirations must necessarily preclude the sort of dénouement associated with mythificational literature.

Puerto América (1940) by Luis María Albamonte is undoubtedly a rather typical example of a dominant strain of Argentine fiction in the early twentieth century: the novel on immigrant themes. [2] Alba-

---

[1] Luis María Albamonte, *Puerto América* (Buenos Aires: A.L.A., Club del Libro Amigos del Libro Americano, 1942).

[2] See the study by Germán García, *El inmigrante en la novela argentina* (Buenos Aires: Librería Hachette, 1970). The following is all García has to say about Albamonte's novel, and it seems to me to place too much emphasis on the rather brief portion of the novel dealing with the countryside: "De

monte's narrative is a thesaurus of the commonplaces of this literature, and it may be read from one point of view as a paean to the
success of immigrants — in this case Italian — in their efforts to
"hacer la América": to make it in America.[3] These commonplaces
include the hardships of the long ocean voyage in cramped, third-class
quarters; the difficulties of separation, usually forever, from parents
and other loved ones and the subsequent pangs of nostalgia for a lost
idyll; the humiliations associated with adjusting to a new environment, an alien culture, and a foreign language; the privations of
life in the *conventillos,* the ghetto-like tenements where many immigrants sank into a lifestyle often less promising than the one left
behind out of the lure of a promised land; all of the traumas attendant upon finding an appropriate place in society and embarking on
a new lifestyle that, it was hoped, would lead, after bitter sacrifices
and blind struggle, to some level of prosperity; and, finally, the
recognition of the first signs of assimilation into Argentine national
life and the occasions for self-congratulation over having, after all
and at last, in effect made it.

The stages in a paradigmatic immigrant experience become the
primary transformations in a narrative scheme that underlies so much
Argentine literature (and, of course, American literature as well) on
the immigrant experience. It may be the basis of a complete textual
elaboration, as it is, in fact, of *Puerto América.* Or a particular
segment of it may serve as the scheme for a text concerned with the
frustration of the final working-out of an ideal, mythified life cycle.
The latter is typically the case in marginal literature like the tango,
the *sainete,* or soap operas, where the failures of the immigrant
experience are the essence of a demythificational stance toward the

---

Buenos Aires trata también especialmente *Puerto América* de Luis María
Albamonte. Es la suya una novela de evocación lírica y en ella nos da la
biografía de un italiano, Luigi Pietra, de sus esperanzas desde el embarque
hasta que, luego de incursiones y excursiones por la campaña, en Buenos Aires
le nace su primer hijo y con él la conciencia de ser ya él mismo argentino.
El campo que conoce Luigi Pietra parece huérfano de criollos, porque extranjeros — italianos como él, judíos, españoles o turcos — son sus compañeros de
fatiga" (p. 64). I have record of no other critical commentary on the novel.
    [3] Albamonte provides the following dedication of his novel: "A mi padre,
médico, nacido en la lejana, desconocida aldea de mis abuelos, muerto en otro
mundo, a cuya tierra le dio generosamente su ciencia, sus sueños y sus huesos,
a cambio de otra maravillosa generosidad: ¡América!" (p. 9).

official shibboleths of the dominant culture. To the extent that Argentina has glorified its immigrant roots and converted them into a national myth, one may expect serious critical and countercultural texts to subject that myth to an unremitting debunking or a least a disinterested questioning.

From Eugenio Cambaceres's *En la sangre* (1887) to Armando Discépolo's expressionistic drama in the teens and twenties — he called them examples of a *grotesco criollo* — there is a solid strain of demythification of the emerging immigrant myth in Argentine culture. This strain is an antiphony to mythificational versions by Alberto Gerchunoff (*Los gauchos judíos,* 1910) or by even such otherwise critical writers as Florencio Sánchez (*La gringa,* 1904) and César Tiempo (*Pan criollo,* 1937), both of whom offered dramatic versions of a positive model of the immigrant experience. (It is perhaps noteworthy that dramatic examples come most immediately to mind; the fact is that I can think of no novel that is as distinguished a creative text on the subject as Sánchez's *La gringa,* his most famous play and the only one of his large production with an optimistic plot resolution, or Discépolo's plays.)

Puerto América does end happily. At least, it ends on the positive note of the protagonist's realization that he has, at last, made a permanent home for himself in Argentina, that he has achieved his goal of prosperity with a restaurant of his own (to which he gives the name that serves as the novel's title), and that with a wife and child he has put down lasting roots in his new home. All of this he accomplishes within the space of ten years from his arrival in 1906. In this sense, Albamonte's novel is a contribution to a group of cultural texts that extol one important version of the immigrant experience in Argentina. Published at a time when the country was moving from a national life dominated by a right-wing government supported by the oligarchy to the sort of mass, populist politics inaugurated by Perón only a few years later, *Puerto América* synthesizes an important sentiment concerning what, by mid-century, had become a major strain of Argentine middle and lower-middle class society: the majority presence in urban centers of immigrants and their immediate descendents.

What makes *Puerto América* of interest to the social realist project of examining critically the bases of Argentine society and of giving voice to those elements that had been marginalized or ignored by elite literature is the way in which the experience of the novel's protagonist is handled. Although Albamonte concludes with a positive image of Luigi Pietra's efforts to make it in America, the novel unflinchingly captures the sufferings and hardships, the spiritual deprivations and compromises that must be made in the pursuit of the elusive promises of success. In what one would presume to be a more characteristically social realist treatment of the immigrant experience, the protagonists would be defeated by social injustice, economic inequities, nonexistent opportunities for material and spiritual fulfillment, and racial and cultural prejudice. In American fiction of the period, this is the texture of James Farrell's *Studs Lonigan* cycle (1935) and Harry Roth's *Call it Sleep* (1934). I know of no Argentine novel of the period to pursue this possibility.

Luigi Pietra experiences a considerable number of setbacks in his pursuit of a vaguely defined success in America. He is appalled by the grubbing lifestyle of his relative's family that takes him in, he is unable for a period to adjust to life in the conventillo and to find work that satisfies him, he seems incapable of making human connections that could result in lasting friendships and sentimental attachments, his fortunes meet many reversals as he discovers that prosperity in the New World is not as easy as it had been made out to be, there is considerable opposition to the immigrants by Creole Argentines (who resent the former's reputation for being more industrious and singleminded in their work than the latter), and he is continually bothered by the self-serving values of his fellow immigrants. Adjustment comes, not surprisingly, with a gradual resignation to these troubling aspects of an inescapable social reality, and Pietra is able to make it, is able to become the novel's prototypic example of the successful immigrant, by assimilating himself to what had initially caused him such anguish. Cheerily cynical in this regard, *Puerto América* shows the protagonist's submerging his sense of guilt at loosing the ties with his family in Italy and accepting the need to provide for himself rather than for them, at transcending his need for love and friendship to adopt the pragmatism of opportunistic decisions, and, finally, accepting the nature of his newfound lifestyle for what it is — typically immigrant Argentina.

The narrative principles of *Puerto América* are based as a consequence on the image of Pietra as a *homo viator,* as a pilgrim who moves through a defined space, undergoes a defined sequence of experiences or adventures, and discovers a defined meaning for his journey. The *homo viator* is also typically a seer, to the extent that he "sees" for us a meaning in a series of paradigmatic experiences. So much pilgrim theme literature — Bunyon's *Pilgrim's Progress* or Baltasar Gracián's *El criticón,* to name a Hispanic example — involves the revelation of meaning for the experiences that the traveler meets along the "highway of life" that, in effect, the narrative trajectory involves presenting to readers situations that are part of their own daily experience. By defamiliarizing them in the context of fiction, the narrator is able to suggest for them a range of meaning readers might not otherwise have associated with them as the normal events of a given social experience. Of course, all literature involves this sort of defamiliarization for purposes of a meaning investiture by the narrator and analytical contemplation by the reader. In the case of those narratives structured around the figure of the *homo viator,* we are dealing with a certain type of experiences structured in terms of movement along a metaphoric path through life.

In the case of *Puerto América,* Pietra's "path" is both spatial and chronological. We see him develop a sense of identity over a ten-year period as he undertakes the Atlantic crossing, installs himself in Buenos Aires, moves from one quarter to another, tries his hand at working as a farm laborer, and finally finds himself as he sets up his own *cantina* back in Buenos Aires. Through his eyes and his consciousness, the reader sees the stations in the journey of the bewildered immigrant seeking his fortune in the New World. It is these stations that are of primary interest for the social realist project of the period. Although Albamonte's narrator is essentially lyrical, in the sense that the recounting of Pietra's experiences and of his states of mind is based on a series of emotional and sentimental metaphors, the representation of the contexts of his experiences deploys the typical rhetorical style of the social realists:

> Hacía quince días que Luigi Pietra había comenzado a trabajar de aprendiz de sastre. Sin embargo, ése no era el oficio con que había soñado. Todo el mundo de su vida se reducía a un banco, un trapo y una aguja. Encerrado entre cuatro paredes, viendo pasar por el patio los verduleros, los proveedores con sus gritos en las bocas, las siluetas humildes y desvalidas de los inquilinos. Él había partido para ir a América. Y América debía ser otra cosa. No aquello, sucio y pobre. No ese silencio o esas grescas entre las mujeres

del conventillo. Ni era el Cumpá, con su párpado caído, ni Salvador con sus silbos, ni Rosa, insinuante y pálida...

América se le escapaba de entre los dedos, desconocida, inubicable, abstracta. Él la había imaginado como una maravillosa materia de ensueño. Más luminosa que su pueblo tendido bajo el sol como un pañuelo recién lavado, más alegre que todas las canciones de los muchachos del prado, más íntima todavía, fascinante. ¿Dónde estaba América? La presentía, cercana, palpitante, como una mujer largamente deseada, escondiéndose caprichosamente en cada sombra, sin huir, pero sin entregarse tampoco. Rondando para exasperar, para hacer sufrir... (p. 83)

This sense of the city, of the experience of socially anonymous individuals whom the novel brings to our attention through the prototypic experiences of its protagonist, and the investment of these experiences with a meaning that identifies them for the reader with a prevailing Argentine sociocultural myth are all aspects of Albamonte's novel that make it of interest for a literary period seeking to redefine the social frame of reference for national culture. *Puerto América* may not be a particularly outstanding novel, but the interplay between an accurate depiction of the harsh social circumstances faced by the millions of immigrants that flooded into Argentina during the fifty-year period between approximately 1880 and 1930 and an overriding perspective that confers upon these experiences a social meaning in the context of the myth of Argentina as an immigrant society provide for an interesting novelistic texture, one that is neither fully consonant with the goals of social realism as denunciatory writing nor yet comfortably inscribed into a completely irreflexive and self-satisfied mythificational culture.

5. JOSÉ RABINOVICH'S JEWISH IMMIGRANTS

José Rabinovich (1903-1978) was undoubtedly one of the most prolific writers on the Jewish immigrant experience in Argentina. Although he published both poetry and drama, [1] the main core of his writing is fiction, both novels and short stories. Born in Russia, a self-taught man and a member of the elite of manual trades in Argentina, the graphic arts, Rabinovich combined an interest in both the proletarian and marginal elements of his society and the often very sorry plight of poor Jews attempting to find a place for themselves in a new country hostile both economically and sociopolitically.

Tercera clase (1944), which was written in Yiddish but published in Spanish, is a series of thirty short fictional pieces prefaced by an enthusiastic introduction signed by Elías Castelnuovo. [2] Castelnuovo

---

[1] Rabinovich's poetry is studied by Naomi Lindstrom, "The Disruptive Poetics of José Rabinovich" (unpublished), and his drama by David William Foster, "Argentine Jewish Dramatists" (unpublished).

[2] Leonardo Senkman, in *La identidad judía en la literatura argentina* (Buenos Aires: Pardes, 1983), makes the following caveat regarding *Tercera clase:* "Se decepcionará quien desee encontrar entre sus artesanos y obreros fracasados la constatación meramente 'sociológica' de una de las facetas más olvidadas de la inmigración judía en la Argentina: el desamparo y la miseria de un vasto sector de trabajadores que vegetaban en el lumpen artesanado sin lograr proletarizarse ni desproletarizarse. Y aquellos que deseen ver simplemente a un exponente del *boedismo* en los relatos de quien garabateaba a tijeretazos de sastre pobre (o con lezna desfilada de zapatero humillado), el dolor obrero de los años 20 y 30 se desentienden del escritor judío que hay en Rabinovich" (p. 107). Senkman's point is well taken: Rabinovich is a writer of the Jewish experience rather than of the proletarian struggle, programmatic or otherwise. My point is simply that the two perspectives coincide in *Tercera clase.* There, the texture of one segment of proletarian life is undeniably portrayed, even if one could wonder why this stratum of the Jewish immigration in Argentina did not receive more extensive treatment by other writers of the period.

sees Rabinovich's writing as the very essense of what, in the more
pompous terms of literary criticism, we may call the social-realist
project:

> Desde este punto de vista José Rabinovich es un artista
> indiscutible. Él no consulta libros para escribir. No lee tra-
> tados de estética para arquitecturar sus obras. No se junta
> con escritores para convenir los términos de su literatura.
> No vive en un ambiente adecuado para promover el refina-
> miento de su instrumental literario. Vive como cualquiera.
> Se da con todos. Hace suyos los problemas de la gente que
> lo rodea. No comulga con el dolor abstracto del arte. Co-
> mulga con el dolor concreto de la vida. Mira el mundo
> como un hombre y lo describe como un hombre. Nunca
> anda preocupado por solucionar cuestiones artísticas. Siempre
> anda preocupado por solucionar cuestiones prácticas. Me
> dice: "Cuando yo visito a un amigo pienso siempre qué es
> lo que le puede faltar a este amigo, y siempre encuentro
> que le falta algo". (pp. 11-12)
> Porque cuando uno lee finalmente lo que este pasajero de
> tercera clase escribe, recibe una impresión inédita. Recibe
> la impresión de que no es un literato el que está relatando
> tales cosas, sino que es un hombre del montón: y cuando
> por fin termina uno de leer eso, sin querer llega a la con-
> clusión de que este hombre del montón lo hace inexplicable-
> mente mejor que un literato. (p. 14)[3]

Clearly, Rabinovich satisfies the imperatives Castelnuovo has expressed in his writings on the demands of proletarian art. [4]

The texts of *Tercera clase* deal essentially with the experiences
of newly arrived immigrants, although a few concern the generational
conflict between immigrant parents and Creole children, while others
are set in the "old country" and deal with the perennial themes of
rural Yiddish writings like cultural values and conflicts between

---

[3] José Rabinovich, *Tercera clase* (Buenos Aires: Editorial Sophos, 1943).
Castelnuovo's introduction has regrettably disappeared from the Barcelona:
Editorial Linosa, 1969 edition of *Tercera clase* (along with the note indicating
that the text was translated into Spanish by Rebeca Mactas de Polak). A
brief "Prólogo" by Ricardo Baeza (pp. 5-7), dated 1946 (and therefore probably
a review notice of the original publication) takes its place.

[4] The postulates of social realist art in Argentina were articulated by Elías
Castelnuovo in *El arte y las masas; ensayos sobre una nueva teoría de la
actividad estética* (Buenos Aires: Colección Claridad, 1935).

Christians and Jews within the pale. The main thrust of the stories is, however, clearly life in the New World: the difficulty of sustaining a sense of Jewish life, Yiddishkeit in a Hispanic context. Argentina has always been an aggressively assimilationist society vis-à-vis what is considered non-Creole. The stories also focus on generational conflict incited by competing social values, the confrontation between the immigrant's dream of a new start and the harsh realities of an alien land, the alienation and despair of individuals who find themselves with no points of reference to give them a secure identity.

These themes concerning the immigrant experience intersect the ones that refer to the marginal lot of those condemned, in Castelnuovo's terms, to live forever in third class. Thus, we find reference to economic exploitation, the insensitivities and cruelties that arise from a hand-to-mouth way of life, the degradation of the human spirit on the fringes of survival, and all of the emotional and psychological conflicts born of the vain attempt to reconcile religious or philosophical ideals with socioeconomic realities.

One of the characteristic notes of the literature on immigrant themes is a nostalgic tone of romantic evocation of the past of one's forefathers. The harshness of this past, while it is typically not ignored, is cushioned by the paean to the nobility of sacrifice on the part of the immigrants and the indomitable spirit that enabled them to survive the shock of economic and sociocultural conflict. The sentimental strain of the folk and the popular of two of the main groups of American immigrants, the Italians and the Jews, provided a framework that enabled the easy idealization of the early immigrant life.

Certainly the Argentine tango, despite all of its references to marginal life, is underlain by a strong current of romantic sentimentality toward immigrant life. But it is perhaps in the *sainete,* an early version of the musical sketch based on Spanish sources but using Argentine lower-middle class themes, where we best see this idealization at work. Alberto Vacarezza's *Tu cuna fue un conventillo* (1920) is unquestionably a gem of this popular Argentine theatrical genre. The tenement house becomes a paradisical space that allows the harmonious integration of every sort of human type and every sort of human conflict.

A text like *Tercera clase,* on the other hand, is a strident repudiation of such cultural artefacts. Rabinovich's goal is to evoke, albeit in the lyrical, measured terms of free indirect style so integral to social realist writing, all of the unremitting harshness and cruelty of his characters' lot. The society thus portrayed is far removed from the edenic fantasies of the sainete, and the basic dynamics of existence and interpersonal contacts serve to degrade human individuals, whose sense of dignity provided by the Judaic tradition and whose sense of moral obligation dictated by Talmudic law are over and over again frustrated, belied, and corrupted by the circumstances of livelihood.

This quality of Rabinovich's stories is to be seen with particular vividness in "Cuando los perros ladran". In place of the prescribed and "natural" respect between fathers and sons, a respect that is an integral part of all societies and religions and not just the Jewish tradition, the story describes the hatred between a father and his young son. Because the former has become an invalid, the son is forced to become the breadwinner of the family. The father hates the son since he is a reminder of the father's inability to provide for his own family. By the same token, the son demands "filial" obeisance from the father in deference to the fact that he has assumed the paternal role. The son, in turn, hates the father both for his having forced him to assume the responsibility of providing for the family and for his refusal to accept the fact that the role of father and son, of provider and dependent, has now been irrevocably reversed. It is this role reversal imposed by the society deficient in its social obligations and the ensuing hatred between father and son which characterize with such pathetic eloquence Rabinovich's vision of Argentine third-class citizens:

> ¿Qué otra cosa justa se hace en el mundo fuera del ladrido de los perros a la luna? ¿Tal vez sea perfectamente natural el hecho de que en la oscura habitación un padre sombrío haga esfuerzos por despertar a su vástago para que éste vaya al trabajo? No es por lástima por lo que hace tales esfuerzos, nada de eso. Ello sería generoso y bello. No. Este padre arranca de su sueño al niño, sin piedad alguna. Mucho le gustaría descender del lecho y con una buena vara hacer saltar al chico de la cama. ¡Con cuánto gusto lo haría! Pero como a él no le es dado hacer las cosas según su gusto, esto también le está vedado. Un gran deseo alienta en su corazón: poder vestirse, lavarse e ir al trabajo. (p. 75)

It is noteworthy that the textual correlative of Rabinovich's vision of immigrants caught in a web of circumstance that both denies their basic humanity and corrupts their traditional Jewish self-identity is to be found in the fact that his narrative voice is so overbearingly expropriative of his characters' own self-image. Throughout he speaks for them with very little in the way of direct dialogue or particularized verbal representation. Moreover, the insistent rhetorical questions establish the characteristic bond between the narrator and the reader, who is asked to assume with the former a sympathetic and understanding stance (whether idealized or unsentimental) toward the lamentable human condition being portrayed. Rabinovich's characters can hardly speak in their own voice for the implacable degradation to which we see them exposed. Hence the image of schizophrenia attributed to the main character of "Patrón," who essentially loses his self-identity in, ironically, realizing the promise of the new land by relinquishing his anarchist ideals in order to fulfill his family's desire to enjoy the prosperity of the small businessman:

> Después de siete años de trabajo en medio de la lana y las chinches, Salmen pareció transfigurado. Pasó por su oficio como un estudiante por la Universidad. El estudiante domina los libros y Salmen se enseñoreó de las lágrimas y la humillación. Surgió en Salmen sin brillo y sin gemido. A veces pensaba, sí en libros, reuniones, huelgas. No sabía a ciencia cierta si los recordaba o si alguien lo había informado sobre estas cosas. Y de pronto, poco a poco, comenzó a distanciarse de aquel Salmen, como de un camarada con el que se ha convivido muchos años y con el cual, de mutuo acuerdo, uno ha resuelto separarse porque no es programa vivir unidos hasta el fin como si fueran dos Salmens. Aquel Salmen, el de los libros, comenzó a alejarse. Con el libro en la mano, le hacía amistosas señas desde lejos; y el otro Salmen, con la máquina de cardar al hombro, correspondía a su saludo sin ninguna pena. Y cuando se quedó solo y sin daño, sintiendo que el otro no le había llevado ningún miembro, devolvió la máquina a quien le pertenecía y retornó muy sosegadamente a su casa. (pp. 151-152)

One linguistic note: *Tercera clase* was originally written in Yiddish, and the Spanish version is a translation by Rebeca Mactas de Polak. Thus, despite Rabinovich's clear commitment to rendering an adequate portrayal of the Buenos Aires immigrant lumpen proletariat and rag-tag shop owners, there is something disquietingly academic about his narrative registers, both the language of the narrator and the language of his characters.[5] Twentieth-century Argentine writing has had a deep sense of obligation to providing a faithful representation of the gritty texture of Buenos Aires urban speech, with its clash of social classes in conflict and kaleidoscopic cultural ideologies in jarring contact.[6] However, the noncolloquial nature of the registers of *Tercera clase* is to be attributed, it seems to me, to the fact that Rabinovich's characters are not speaking Spanish but rather Yiddish: the narrator's free indirect style becomes thus an extension of the Yiddish rather than Hispanic world inhabited by the characters of the stories. As a consequence, the noncolloquial nature of Rabinovich's prose can in no way be said to detract from the unremitting antiidealization and antisentimentality with respect to immigrant life that the author undertakes to portray.

[5] Senkman refers (p. 116), with respect to *Tercera clase,* to Rabinovich's "acústica continental," attributing the categorization to Ricardo Baeza via César Tiempo's "Un diálogo con José Rabinovich," in *El perro de Maidenek* (La Plata: Platense, 1968), p. 10.

[6] Concerning the representation of colloquial registers in Argentine literature, see Nélida E. Donni de Mirande, *La lengua coloquial y la lengua de la literatura argentina* (Rosario: Universidad Nacional del Litoral, Cuadernos del Instituto de Letras, 1967).

III. TOWARD A CRITICAL CONSCIOUSNESS

6. THE FORMATION OF A CRITICAL ARGENTINE CONSCIOUSNESS IN BERNARDO VERBITSKY'S *EN ESOS AÑOS*

> Sentía que su propia personalidad maduraba si-
> multáneamente con el conocimiento razonado de su
> país, la Argentina, pero ambos procesos no impor-
> taban a nadie. El país sólo podía madurar bajo las
> actuales condiciones no porque fueran las mejores,
> sino porque dejaban un margen a la evolución.
> (p. 339) [1]

With the death of Bernardo Verbitsky (1907-1978), Argentina lost one of its truly prolific men of letters. The author of over a dozen massive and far-ranging novels, Verbitsky set the tone for a number of writers in twentieth-century Argentine fiction concerned with sweeping, complex interpretations of the sociocultural bases of Argentina. [2] Writers like Ernesto Sábato (1911-), David Viñas (1929-), Héctor A. Murena (1921-1975) are only three names of writers who to one degree or another owed a debt to Verbitsky for providing a

---

[1] Bernardo Verbitsky, *En esos años* (Buenos Aires: Editorial Futuro, 1947).
[2] Basic references on Verbitsky's writing are José Barcia, "Bernardo Verbitsky," in Pedro Orgambide, and Roberto Yanhi, *Enciclopedia de la literatura
argentina* (Buenos Aires: Editorial Sudamericana, 1970), pp. 616-618; Juan
F. Bazán, "Bernardo Verbitsky," in his *Narrativa paraguaya y latinoamericana*
(Asunción, 1976), pp. 215-221; Juan Carlos Martini Real, "Los libros de Bernardo Verbitsky," *Macedonio*, Nos. 6-7 (1970), 67-77; and Carlos Mastrágelo,
"Bernardo Verbitsky: novelista porteño," *Ficción*, No. 10 (1957), 52-60. Verbitsky is included in Kessel Schwartz, "The Jew in Twentieth-Century Argentine
Fiction," *The American Hispanist*, No. 19 (1977), 9-12.

model of the detailed fictional treatment of current national events and international happenings as they impinged on Argentine national life. Like his contemporary Eduardo Mallea (1903-1981) — and despite the fact that the proletariat and Jewish Verbitsky had little in common with the aristocratic and Catholic Mallea in terms of background and ideology — Verbitsky assumed wholeheartedly and without reservations the imperative to provide in his novels a detailed analysis of the texture of life at specific moments in modern Argentine social history. [3]

En esos años (1947) is exemplary of both Verbitsky's novelistic project and of the revisionist program of the social realist in Argentina of which he was one outstanding representative. Four-hundred pages of small-print text cover the period stretching from the Treaty of Munich to near the end of 1942. Although, of course, the war did not touch Buenos Aires directly, Argentina received a steady stream of immigrants and refugees, beginning with the Civil War in Spain in the thirties. By the time Verbitsky published his novel, Nazi refugees had already arrived in the country, and Perón's interest in them, both because of his own ideological leanings and because of opportunities to do business on the basis of Argentine passports, had already begun to become public knowledge. Finally, the interest of Buenos Aires's considerable Jewish community in the fate of German and East European Jews enhanced Argentina's normally acute concern over European affairs, which are followed in that country with a level of interest unparalleled in Latin America as a whole.

Verbitsky's novel is based on the representation of the tremendous preoccupation with the war in Argentina, particularly in Buenos Aires, with its millions of immigrants and sons and daughters of immigrants, its extensive commercial ties to Europe, and the fundamental conviction that the Argentine metropolis is a far-flung European capital. The overall narrative basis of *En esos años* is a series of

---

[3] Fernando Alonso and Arturo Rezzano appropriately accord Verbitsky a prominent place in their *Novela y sociedad argentinas* (Buenos Aires: Editorial Paidós, 1971), "Bernardo Verbitsky," pp. 150-161: "Sin duda es Bernardo Verbitsky uno de los principales exponentes de la novelística social del 40" (p. 150). Juan Carlos Portantiero is considerably less charitable, and virtually dismisses Verbitsky as part of the *atraso* of the lingering Boedo frame of reference well into the 1940s: *Realismo y realidad en la narrativa argentina* (Buenos Aires: Ediciones Procyón, 1961), p. 77 passim.

meditations, conversations, and expositions of various complementary and contradictory opinions held by Argentines and Europeans in Argentina concerning the emerging events of the war.[4] Although written a few years after the close of hostilities, *En esos años* does not involve the ironic flashback coloring of the presentation of these concerns. That is, the narrator does not frame them with subsequent opinion based on the final outcome of the war, although it is natural that the reader follow the many references to political and military fortunes with an understanding of how they tally with the European situation toward the end of the decade. A uniformity of tone is maintained in the representation of the attempts to comprehend and to come to terms with the day-to-day chronology of events on the part of a broad cross-section of the urban Argentine middle class.

Like so many of Verbitsky's novels, *En esos años* brings together a representative cast of Argentine individuals. Generally speaking, the characters of these novels are solidly middle class, exemplars of the successful if not problem-free emergence of a predominantly middle-class urban society in Argentina. Typically, Verbitsky's characters are young marginal professionals — the large majority, as in the case of this novel, are newspapermen and would-be writers. To a great degree, Verbitsky's characters are doppelgangers of their creator (as Mallea's central characters in work after work are doubles of the novelist as the paradigmatic "invisible Argentine" of which they are just so many interlocking facets), and it would be stretching a point to say that Verbitsky was ever very concerned about creating characters with any sense of fully rounded, autonomous personalities; more on this aspect of his writing below.

Thus, a Verbitsky novel is a vast mosaic, a series of relatively short chapters — although there may be some fairly long segments based on debates or dialogues between individuals representing contrasting points of view about a certain issue. Often the reader has the distinct impression that there is little happening in the romance sense of action and reaction, and there is certainly little of substance

---

[4] Germán García calls *En esos años* "[una] especie de película hecha con las noticias que fueron llegando sobre la revuelta española": *La novela argentina* (Buenos Aires: Editorial Sudamericana, 1952), p. 231. I have no idea why García refers only to news about the Spanish Civil War, which occupies only the first third of the novel, the bulk of the text being devoted to Nazi aggression in East Europe and Russia and over London.

for the reader interested in finely drawn psychological portraits. There is the flow and flux of individuals coming together, talking, and separating, and there is the elaborate texture of the crisscross of contrapuntal dialogue on the one hand and of meandering interior monologues on the other. The reader looking for the romance or the psychological novel may well wonder to what extent the cast of characters in a Verbitsky novel has personal traits to distinguish them from one another or why, beyond readily identifiable sociopolitical positions, there is any need for character differentiation at all. For example, characters are readily identified as the supporters of the Germans vs. the supporters of the Allies, the supporters of the Loyalists vs. the supporters of Franco, the supporters of a Germanic Europe vs. the supporters of a Catholic/Romanic Europe, the supporters of democratic traditions vs. the supporters — themselves ranged into opposing camps — of fascist and communist ideologies. Nevertheless, as I develop in the following comments, it is essentially incorrect to question the novelistic coherence of *En esos años*. [5]

What holds a novel like *En esos años* together is the presence of a controlling consciousness, one that superficially can easily be taken as the surrogate of the author as a self-conscious and publically defined Argentine citizen. Pedro Lascano serves this function in the novel under examination. It is his personal story, his relationship and subsequent marriage to Mariana, and his experiences as a newspaper reporter and editorialist and as an aspiring writer that serve as the unifying and personal point of reference for the frieze of events, opinions, and position-takings in the novel. Although the concept has been overused, it would be appropriate to speak of Pedro as a "hero" in the sense of Georg Lukács's definition of the historical novel. [6] For Lukács, this hero is the focal point for a

---

[5] As Alonso and Rezzano do: "[es] una obra segura en su realización, provista de un mensaje humano muy hondo y en la que su autor, olvidándose a veces de mantener las formas del género, incursiona a modo de ensayo y hasta como con cámaras fotográficas, por entre los senderos que los días del 37 al 42 ofrecían en Buenos Aires" (pp. 152-153).

[6] Georg Lukács, *The Historical Novel*, trans. by Hannah and Stanley Mitchell (Boston: Beacon Press, 1963, c1962): "We see how a deep involvement with society and with an individual's tasks therein make for the type of the 'World-historical individual', in whom both the individual's involvement with his social work, his absorption therein, as well as the extensive and intensive significance of this task appear at their highest point" (p. 103).

coherently defined social consciousness. Through the specific adventures and character modifications he undergoes, the reader perceives the elaborate panorama of specific time and place in the social and cultural terms of materialistic history. A concrete example — a *typus* or figure — of historical processes as they impinge upon human individuals, the Lukácsian hero represents to the reader the complex outlines and sense of those processes. In the process the hero may perceive for himself the meaning of his experiences, but in all cases he serves as the opportunity for the reader to achieve a depth of understanding and a sense of the rich texture of social meaning.

In Verbitsky's novels, the characters who serve as the organizing axis of consciousness are in the process of comprehending their own attempts at comprehension. That is, they are existentially conscious individuals for whom the entire meaning of existence is an act of self-analysis and a conscientious striving for understanding of themselves, of their position in the Argentine sociocultural fabric, and of the characteristic design of that fabric. Verbitsky's characters may not satisfy the canonical existential suffering of the tormented soul or the Sartrean imperative to all-defining gestures of action: Verbitsky's frame of reference remains too solidly the proletarian model of the "decent" individual who in dealing with the injustices and the hypocrisies of social and political institutions articulates, if only by implication, an appropriately socially-redeeming posture toward them. In the case of Pedro, this posture corresponds to the pattern of the freedom fighter, the humanitarian and libertarian, the defender of Western democratic institutions but with considerable sympathy for the spirit of the Popular Front, the proponent of the Judeo-Christian tradition of the redemption of man as opposed to the primitive forces of destruction that underpin the values of Hitler's Reich. This may all be a bit of an ideological mishmash, but it corresponds well to the general sentiments of the independent radicals of the period. In Argentina, these were the sentiments of those who both were opposed to the triumph of fascism in Europe in the persons of Franco, Hitler, and Mussolini and who were opposed to the successive military governments in Argentina of the thirties and early forties and of the subsequent emergence of the Peronista movement.

Pedro Lascano, therefore, is the point of confluence for a series of overlapping feelings and values in favor of a socially redemptive

society that Verbitsky subscribed to and promoted through the eloquence of his novels. And Pedro serves also as the corrective point
of reference for a variegated array of destructive, benighted, antihu-
manitarian/antilibertarian principles that often unfortunately seem
to hold sway in the turbulent panorama of events Verbitsky is at
pains to depict. In the sort of indirect free style that allows the
narrative voice to assume the guise of the interior monologue or
preverbal consciousness of the characters, the following passage is
typical of the conscious self-evaluation Pedro and the other characters who are essentially his satellites engage in:

> Había sido un largo aprendizaje, una difícil marcha, pero la
> llegada a ese mirador deparaba un panorama que no muchos
> sospechaban. Esto no significaba que perdiera de vista su
> próximo paisaje cotidiano. Todo lo contrario. Pero sabía
> armonizar la visión de uno y otro plano, reconstituyendo
> la realidad en la minucia política, el espectáculo callejero,
> la modalidad social, la estructura económica, en el acuerdo
> de los estadistas y en la denuncia de los tratados. Y con-
> templaba a cada uno de los días plenos en la totalidad de
> una novela cuyos capítulos no se componían de la suma de
> lo ocurrido sino de la textura ordenada de los sucesos. Menos
> sencillo que enumerar los hechos ya ocurridos, fue vivirlos
> hilando conjeturas en torno a sus posibilidades, fue sentirse
> defraudado por cierto rumbo de los acontecimientos (ha-
> berse sentido pisotear veinte mil veces su injusticia). No
> basta hablar de cables. Leer cables de cierta manera es con-
> vertirse en el testigo de la historia. Pero enteramente pasivo,
> pues de nada podía servir su dolorosa impotencia. Era apren-
> der a morir más lúcidamente, y nada más. (p. 60)

The operative words in this passage — so typical of the overall
texture of *En esos años* and, indeed, of Verbitsky's writings as a
unified whole — are *aprendizaje, mirador, contemplar, conjeturas,
aprender*. For the entire sense of this narrative is based on the attempt, the result in turn of a deeply felt imperative, of the focal
character to attain an adequate level of understanding of his social
milieu. This understanding is the product of a long and arduous
process of constructing a coherent interpretation based on circumstantial facts and conjectures, and it constitutes in its totality both a
loss of innocence and an apprenticeship in social commitment that
gives meaning to a personal consciousness, an individual sense of

meaningful existence. This is, in its most fundamental terms, a variant of a quest motif, where the object of the quest is not some symbolic material object (e.g., prototypically the Holy Grail or some other object invested with deep mythic significance), but knowing as a coherent structure of human thought.

Grasping the unifying patterns of *En esos años* becomes, therefore, an investigation of the textual strategies for, on the one hand, underscoring Pedro's quest for meaning and understanding and, on the other, the means by which Verbitsky's obvious "editorializing" interest in discussing the humanistic issues of the war are given some sort of fictional investiture. The first principle relates to the sustaining coherence of Pedro (as well as certain other satellite characters) as a human lens on social history, while the latter principle concerns the way in which the novelist fulfills the entire project of his writing career of using fiction as a vehicle for the analysis of social history. Pedro as an evolving consciousness emphasizes the need to see the processes of history in terms of their impact on individual, personalized human beings, and *En esos años* contains some interesting material with reference to the Aristotelian validation of "poetry" (i.e., creative or fictive writing) as a superior form of knowledge. And Pedro as the focal point of the narrative confirms, within an internationalist perspective of Argentine culture, the need to translate foreign affairs into a program for the adequate formation of a national social consciousness.

If the novel is viewed as primarily of interest for the intersection of monumental historical events and a modest and self-conscious individual, a man who sees himself as a modest journalistic and literary scrivener, it becomes appropriate to investigate the dominant strategies of the narrative for framing or highlighting the ways in which Pedro takes stock of his historical situation and attempts to assign an interpretive meaning to it.

The most insistent pattern toward this end is the extensive array of prefatory tags that underscore Pedro's interpretive attempts. These tags, in syntactic terms, are higher predicates — that is, opening verbal phrases — that contain, as their direct complement nominal clauses, a proposition of interpretation. Moreover these tags operate in an anaphoric fashion throughout the novel, to the extent that blocks of text that constitute Pedro's analysis of events are prefaced by one and another of these tags. Admittedly, we are dealing here with the sort of concentrated repetition to be found in poetry, where successive lines begin with a similar phrase or network of phrases. Nonetheless, the stylistic diffuseness of a four-hundred page novel cannot mask the fact that Pedro's interior monologues are invariably introduced — syntactically cued might be a more accurate description of these patterns — by phrases that highlight how the substantive interpretations that follow are but part of his own mental process and of the evolution of his personal consciousness. These tags, by the same token, are not part of the substantive analytical meditations, but are, rather, a sort of discursive punctuation that reminds the reader that material which is made up of stretches of political analysis, is, above all else, part of an individual human perception of meaning.

These tags take some of the following forms: *pensaba que, sentía que* (undoubtedly the two most recurring phrases in this respect), *creía que, se dio cuenta de que, entendió que, se decía que.* All of these phrases belong to the pattern "Pedro *thought* (etc.) that X," where X represents the substantive matter of Pedro's interpretive efforts. Such a pattern accomplishes the goal of installing a socio-historical issue within the consciousness of a fictional character who has the distinction of possessing a high degree of typicity in terms of the sort of modest but nevertheless heroic humanistic stance toward the remote events that impinge on the everyday lives of common people:

> Pedro sentía que todo intento de interpretación de los hechos de hoy estaba modelado por ideas fijas que dejó la otra guerra. Resultaba difícil pensar en una guerra corta. Tampoco estaba entreviendo que pudiera ser larga. Nada resultaba claro. Había tal vez, en medio de todo, una absurda complaciencia profesional, periodística. En las películas norteamericanas, sobre todo en las "cabalgatas" retrospectivas podían verse los títulos enormes que publicaron los diarios yanquis al iniciarse la guerra en el 14 o al entrar los Estados Unidos en el 17. Las letras de WAR ocupaban media página. Esperábase quizá la ocasión de hacer aquí lo mismo. Llegó. Y en su diario apareció el título GUERRA alto como un estallido. O como un grito de alivio.
>
> Vagamente admitía Pedro que había finalizado la etapa que crispaba los nervios. Y dominaba un temor: que se

usara gases asfixiantes, y un interrogante: el de Rusia, dueña
al parecer de sus nervios, alzándose a un costado de los
acontecimientos, fría, impasible. (p. 88)

While it must be borne in mind that the text in almost its
totality is made up of disquisitions such as this one, such that the
political and military events of the war are veritably chronicled in
Verbitsky's novel, it should be obvious from this representative
quote how much discourse can be appended to the tags that open
the two paragraphs (*sentía que* and *admitía que,* respectively). Other
tags obeying different syntactic configurations are also involved, one
of which appears in two guises in this quote: *quizá* and *tal vez.*
Such parenthetical qualifiers also do not belong to the substantive
propositional meaning of Pedro's analysis; they are, rather, subjective tags that link the discourse with a mediating consciousness
that is engaged in the process of framing and qualifying the facts
being rehearsed. These tags are, in sum, part of a personal interpretation of the sense of the facts and issues. Other predicates,
whether in the form of verbal phrases (*difícil pensar que, dominaba
un temor ... que,* or adverbial qualifiers like *vagamente* fulfill
precisely the same function. Thus, even though the phrase "Nada
resultaba claro" is unaccompanied by the customary so-called "dative
of interest," there can be little question that the one for whom
these questions lack clarity is Pedro, the unspecified *le* about whose
attempts at interpretation this phrase punctuates.

Another dominant textual strategy is that of the rhetorical
question, whether preceded or not by the prefatory tag *se preguntó
si* or its numerous possible variants. Like the prefatory tags discussed
above, theoretical questions constitute a further device for "disengagement," whereby the thematic concerns that the reader is able
to attribute to the narrator on the basis of the latter's transitional
articulations are transferred to Pedro as part of his internalized
preoccupations.[7] Quite simply, Pedro raises with himself the pertinent questions relating to the overall thematic concerns of the novel,
and his meditations, analyses, and interpretations are all part of his
attempt to answer satisfactorily these questions. Furthermore, to the

---

[7] For a more extensive definition of the concept of disengagement, see
A. J. Greimas, and J. Courtés, *Semiotics and Language; An Analytical Dictionary* (Bloomington: Indiana University Press, 1982), pp. 87-91.

extent that other satellite characters in the novel also engage in similar attempts at understanding, whether along the same lines as Pedro does or out of some conflicting sociopolitical commitment, their interior monologues are likewise characterized by the positing of rhetorical questions that are to be "replied to" in the due course of their ruminations.

It would be possible to subcategorize these questions and to derive distinctions like *ironic questions* (those in which the narrator implies the answer but to which the character must nevertheless duly respond), *self-evident questions* (to which a response is already apparent by virtue of the general humanistic commitment of the text), *summary questions* (of the nature "Isn't this after all what is meant by . . . ," such that the answer to the question synthesizes the line of thought up to that point), *"existential" questions* (those that demand a response beyond the ken of limited human resources, such as the why and to what purpose of destructive human behavior, injustice, and cynical human nature), or *"aleatory" questions* that relate a particular circumstance to a series of unknown factors regarding the human condition or a given political condition. One could also speak of questions with the thrust of an *adynaton* — that is, the expression of a questionably attainable state ("Wouldn't it be nice if," "Why can't it be that"). These and other syntactically interrogative constructions punctuate the flow of text and frame the responses to them as attempts attributable to specific fictional individuals to come to terms with the overall thematic concerns of the novel. The overlapping, complementary, contradictory, and antiphonic responses of Pedro in the first instance and the satellite characters to a lesser degree constitute the specifically narrative and fictive nature of the text, despite whatever extent to which one may be tempted to attribute to it an essayistic nature based on the clear way in which it is circumscribed by the sociopolitically committed themes of the time in which it was published.

It is noteworthy the degree to which the sorts of rhetorical questions I have described dot the pages of the novel. Surely, since it would be difficult to argue that one organizes thoughts in this question-and-answer format, such a textual feature is characteristically and self-consciously "literary" in a fashion one would not find in a novel purporting to transcribe with a sense of authenticity the preverbal stream of consciousness of human thought. In other words, passages like the following are stylistically very mannered, and it is features such as these rhetorical questions that give Verbitsky's prose its very dense quality. Disengagements like these may move the editorializing toward the realm of the fictive, but they also give the impression, as a consequence of the antinaturalistic format of the Socratic dialogue, of the most thinly veiled of novelized essays:

> Sí, esas palabras, masacre, exterminio, que se me gastan. ¿De qué sirve toda esta literatura que yo y otros hemos prodigado en el diario de ayer, 31 de mayo? Y después de este espanto que sólo podemos concebir, durante un instante aislado, que sólo nos representamos en un único minuto, un momento de inspiración dentro de la lectura, ¿cómo haremos todos para proseguir una literatura hecha de palabras? Sí. Es cada vez más para mí un problema éste de escribir. Harto de palabras, avergonzado de emplearlas, convencido de su inutilidad y al mismo tiempo entreviendo que por el camino del oficio se puede llegar al odio que se supone vocación. Y por sentirlo en esta mañana más fuertemente que nunca, tanto menos deseo decirlo en el estilo posible. ¿Después que esto pase —si alguna vez pasa— se volverá a la literatura de siempre? (p. 108)

> ¿Qué es posible hacer entonces del hombre, orgullosa criatura que dispone aparentemente de su razón y su intuición? Porque evidentemente la suprema perversidad de los nazis se manifestaba fundamentalmente en su obra de deformación íntima del individuo. Y Pedro sintió en ese momento que el asombro y el pavor de una revelación le traspasaba verticalmente: entonces, el hombre, ¿no tiene defensa? ¿No hay en él vallas naturales que rechacen la brutalización? (p. 212)

The debate or dialogue format is, of course, a type of text whose prestige extendes back to classical Greek and Roman literature, and there are examples throughout Western literature that confirm its vitality as an appropriate textual format for contrasting and comparing differing points of view. Embodying these points of view in different characters or groups of characters is simply another form of discursive disengagement by which other voices are distinguished from that of the controlling narrator, who may simply recede or disappear from the text, with one or another of the fictive "debators" charged with carrying the burden of a privileged point of view. In Hispanic literature, the complex and ironic conversations between

Don Quixote and Sancho Panza are merely one striking variant of this textual mode.

Given the multiple sociopolitical issues involved with the thirties and forties in Europe and the fact that Verbitsky's long text gives these issues full play through Pedro's meditations on them and his contacts with individuals — Argentines and exiles — who embody them in all their various nuances, it is only natural that the long blocks of text that consist of the interior monologues of Pedro and other characters be interspersed with circumstantial conversations, dialogues, debates, and verbal duels in places like the editorial room of *La tarde* (the daily for which Pedro writes), in cafés, bars, and restaurants, in literary and cultural soirées, and in political meetings (of particular note are the sessions of the center for exiled Republican Spaniards in Buenos Aires, named after the great novelist Benito Pérez Galdós). These textual examples are too extensive to quote for illustrative purposes. Suffice it to say that they also contribute to the general sense of the novel as a text focusing on the development of a specifically committed form of human consciousness.

Pedro's profession as a newspaperman and his aspirations to becoming a creative writer provide a particularly eloquent example of the complexity of his attempts to interpret adequately his historical situation. In the course of the novel, in addition to the newspaper articles and editorials he composes, we are given information about political essays he writes, about a drama he has produced (without much success), about several short stories he has written, and about a five hundred page novel that he doggedly attempts to place. The difficulties and frustrations that he has in the latter regard, along with the failure of his theatrical work to strike a responsive chord among critics and the public, provide the opportunity for some incidental sarcastic and rueful observations about the nature of literary activity at the time of *En esos años;* moreover, Pedro, in defending the nature of his own novel, also provides a defense for precisely the sort of novel of which he is the main character — undoubtedly Verbitsky's earnest desire to forestall any criticism his own work might receive as too "journalistic" or too "essayistic" or too "obsessed with current events."

Throughout the novel, there is a binary opposition between images of life and images of death. Consonant with the interpretation of Nazism as related to chthonic forces, with primitive and pre-

Christian Germanic traditions, and with the mythology of Wotan, Pedro repeatedly meditates on how the culture of Hitler's Germany has harnessed a panoply of destructive forces in the human psyche and in society. Concomitantly, the only forms of art and literature possible under Nazism are those related to values associated with conceptual primes like mayhem, hatred, destruction, and death. Although this sort of image has come to be the accepted interpretation sustained by the Allied victors in the war against Hitler — indeed, one has had to accept the flourishing of an appalling kitsch cultural industry thriving on the marketing of endlessly repeated variations of the Nazi horror, a veritable SM fantasy in its most specious forms — Pedro's interpretation in a novel published in Latin America barely two years after the fall of Germany (and at the time of the rise of a fascistic Peronismo) has an immediacy lacking in present-day trivialized accounts:

> No sabe el mundo qué legiones ha lanzado Hitler. Fanatizar el pueblo con hogueras de libros, señalar a los intelectuales como los causantes de la suprema humillación del país. Es infernal. Es especular sobre las fuerzas del mal no vencidas, y evocarlas, para ponerlas a su servicio. ¡Sutilizar luego sobre si el pueblo alemán sigue o no a Hitler! Un breve margen de opción pudo quedar a los que por su edad no eran catequizables. Pero idiotizados, muchos vieron la única posibilidad de imponer sus sueños fracasados de socialismo. (pp. 345-346).

While American popular culture during the war maintained a united front against Germany as part of the involvement of the United States in the European theater, it must be borne in mind that Argentina maintained official neutrality until the very end of the war and that many elements in that country among both the citizenry and foreign exiles were proud to announce their sympathy for either the German cause, the Italian cause, or both. Although Pedro is not a Jew, the second most represented consciousness in the novel is that of a Jew, Pedro's fellow journalist and aspiring writer, Enrique Goldberg. It is only natural that Verbitsky, as one of the most committed Jewish writers of his generation, define clearly an anti-Nazi position. [8] As a consequence, the plight of the

---

[8] On Jewish themes in Verbitsky's writings, see Leonardo Senkman, *La identidad judía en la literatura argentina* (Buenos Aires: Editorial Pardes, 1983),

Jews in Europe during the war and Argentina's less than praise-
worthy behavior toward Jews seeking refuge constitute an important
subplot parallel to the overall negative description of Hitler's sociocultural programs.

In terms of the binary opposition between life and death, literature becomes for Pedro an element of life and redemption, despite
his frequent despair over the efficacy of literature in a modern
society so bent on the destruction of human dignity and human
values. Paralleling the images of Hitler's destruction of culture,
Pedro's thoughts envision a literature capable of restoring humanitarian sentiments:

> ¿Y si enloqueciese de pronto y convencido, obsesionado,
> persiguiese en furiosa creación un poema cuya clarinada in-
> movilice la guerra? Detener todos los gestos de la guerra,
> llevar la paz al corazón. ¿Un poema? Escrito con una ame-
> tralladora, tal vez. Olvidó esta fantasía y retomando lo an-
> terior llegó a la conclusión de que su discutirse a sí mismo,
> su largo cavilar, era el modo de inquirir acerca de la natu-
> raleza del impulso del escritor. Y en ese mismo instante se
> dio una respuesta: era la forma más clara que en él tomaba
> el deseo de vivir, el amor a la vida. (p. 229)

Pedro has no starry-eyed visions about the possibility of combat-
ing tanks and bombs with poems. Indeed, as a journalist who daily
reads the reports of the implacable progress of the war and the
suffering of anonymous individuals in the path of its machinery, he
experiences periods of intense pessimism and despair, wondering real-
istically about how he will adjust to a German victory that could
well mean the installation of Germanic supremacy in Argentina and
Latin America (as a matter of fact, one of his colleagues, an ardent
supporter of Hitler, taunts him to this effect, cruelly promising
that he will, however, be saved from the concentration camp).

By contrast, the points of reference of the meditations represented by these two quotes, rather than representing a movement
toward the resolution of Pedro's feelings in terms of either hope

---

"Verbitsky, o la crispación de la identidad judía," pp. 365-374. See also Stephen
A. Sadow, "*Judíos y gauchos:* The Search for Identity in Argentine Jewish
Literature," *American Jewish Archives*, 34 (1982), 164-177; Verbitsky is dis-
cussed on pp. 173-177.

or despair, constitute an important axiological opposition in the novel that accounts for a large number of textual fragments: Pedro's interior monologues, his conversations with his wife, his activities as a writer which are incorporated directly and indirectly into the text of *En esos años,* and dialogues and debates with an array of professional and political individuals with whom he interacts in the course of four hundred pages of narrative.

Perhaps the most interesting embodiment of the disjunction death through war and life through literature is in the work he sketches for his wife in response to the cables describing the dreadful bombing of London, the blackouts, the cramped bomb shelters, and the small acts of heroism of a people in the face of the constant elements of violent death. The result is a segment of the text in which Pedro senses himself as a participant in the disaster and not merely a detached Latin American journalist who, thousands of miles removed from the scene of the bombings, manages to imagine a full range of details on the basis of the frozen words of agency cables:

> Pedro dejó el diario, pero durante unos minutos aún siguió viviendo en aquella caverna entre cuyas sombras se disimulaba la vida [i.e., the bomb shelter]. Imaginaba las familias con sus chicos. Duermen los pibes abrazados a las madres, rodeando su cuello con los bracitos. Un sueño pesado hace homogénea esa masa humana en el extenso subsuelo. Y sobre ese gran mitin horizontal flota un cálido tufo. Mitin horizontal no convocado por ningún fervor, ni siquiera por un entusiasmo como en el fútbol, sino por el miedo y el desaliento, no para gritar juntos, sino para echarse juntos, pero en la soledad incomunicada de cada uno, para llorar silenciosamente hacia adentro, para velar y para maloler juntos. (p. 175)

Thus, Pedro's emotional involvement with the details of the impact of the war on ordinary human beings — the Jews of Germany, Poland, and other countries invaded by Hitler; the Englishmen subjected to nightly bombings — is transformed into one of the major textual strategies of Verbitsky's novel. As part of Pedro's concern for human life and for the forces and values that sustain it, his meditations, interpretations, and analyses assume the form of the recreation of the horrible reality of war. As a consequence, *En esos años* is a literary text that portrays the interior monologue text of an individual who recreates in his thoughts the "social text" of the European war.

It is this embedded configuration for the various texts in the discourse of the novel — fleshed out by journalistic texts and literary texts, which are incorporated either directly by full quotation or indirectly by summary in the words of the narrator or one of the characters — that lends *En esos años* its density as a consideration of the nature of World War II and the humanitarian/humanistic issues it raised. The final confirmation of the importance of this array of textual perspectives is their importance for the formation of an appropriate Argentine consciousness. Where it is clear that for many Argentines the military theaters of the war far removed from Argentina and irrelevant to the daily life of the country (which at the time was emerging from the military dictatorships inaugurated by Uriburu's fascist overthrow in 1930 and moving toward the triumph of Peron's political ambitions), for Pedro there is no aspect of the war that does not impinge upon his concerns as an Argentine citizen. The values in conflict in the war; the public and the private political machinations of official, semiofficial and extraofficial agents; the implications of the parties of the war for Argentina's Spanish, Italian, French, English, and Jewish cultural roots; the presence in the country of sympathizers for various ideologies in conflict and the institutional history of the country since 1930 are all features of Pedro's preoccupation and obsessions, not as an idly curious professional journalist assigned to cover the day-to-day events of the war, but as an Argentine who feels himself obliged to assimilate these events in terms of their implication for his own life and for the life of his fellow countrymen. Any initial impulse to ironic detachment is counterbalanced by the realization of an inescapable international involvement:

> Enrique, a solas consigo mismo, en el amarillento final de la noche, incorporaba los telegramas al noticiario, en medio de una gran confusión de espíritu. Ante el destino de esas gentes, podía quizá responder con una sonrisa de incredulidad y hasta con una carcajada de impotencia. (pp. 48-59)

> Estamos un poco lejos y no tenemos guerra, y mientras en cada noche en Europa, los pueblos mueren, agonizan, se apagan en medio del sufrimiento, aquí sigue la fiesta sin

modificaciones. Y unos cuantos vivos ensayan imitaciones de führers y se aprovechan de esa desorientación que nuestra vida lleva, para convertir en número, a cada componente de este desfile sin rumbo. Fútbol, baile, pasear por Corrientes, llenar los cines. Nada nos pertenece, ni el presente, ni el pasado ni el porvenir. Nada se resuelve entre nosotros y el problema que me planteo acerca de lo que yo [i.e., Pedro] puedo hacer personalmente por la solución de los problemas del mundo, que me repercuten, se vincula directamente a mis temas de preocupación: comprender el país. Y en el detalle, entender la relación capital-provincia, las relaciones del país con el exterior. (p. 250)

Unquestionably, it is this sort of commitment, elaborated in *En esos años* through the extensive array of textual strategies that I have described, that attests amply to Verbitsky's interpretation of the imperative of social realism in Argentina.

7. MAX DICKMANN'S *MADRE AMÉRICA:* A REFRACTED IMAGE OF THE *DÉCADA INFAME*

> Es la vida grande y abierta, es la vida del cuerpo
> y del alma sin más trabas que las de la misma
> naturaleza, es lo mejor de sí mismo que va dejando
> atrás en la estela del agua...; sí, lo mejor de sí
> mismo; su vida desprovista de todo control, porque
> la vida así es sangre y es drama. (p. 80) [1]

It is difficult to attribute to the best-known work of Max Dickmann (1902-) a direct filiation with the novel of social protest and social realism in Argentina. [2] Although Dickmann is one of the Spanish-language translators of Erskine Caldwell, a key figure in American

---

[1] Max Dickmann, *Madre América;* edición conmemorativa 1935-1960 (Buenos Aires: Santiago Rueda-Editor, 1960).

[2] There are two valuable critical monographs on Dickmann's writing. Héctor P. Agosti, *Las novelas de Max Dickmann* (Buenos Aires: Claridad, 1939?), emphasizes Dickmann's interest in the emerging petite bourgeoisie at the expense of the old landed gentry. In my opinion, he inflates Dickmann's narrative skills, but he does provide an accurate description of seven dominant techniques in the novels (pp. 40-41). Amando J. Cobo, *¿A dónde va la literatura argentina? La novela: redescubrimiento de Max Dickmann* (Buenos Aires: Ediciones de Losange, 1954), provides a general characterization based on Dickmann's own assertion that "La Argentina real se parece a la descrita en mis libros" (p. 7). See also the following notes: Francisco Herrera, "Max Dickmann," in Roberto Yahni, and Pedro Orgambide, *Enciclopedia de la literatura argentina* (Buenos Aires: Editorial Sudamericana, 1970), p. 190; Alberto Lasplaces, "La novela en América. A propósito de la novela de Max Dickmann, 'Madre América'," *Nosotros,* 2.ª época, No. 4 (1936), 372-383; Enrique Mallea Abarca, "Variaciones sobre una novela de Max Dickmann [*Frutos amargos*]," *Nosotros,* 2.ª época, No. 74 (1942), 301-312; Ethel Kuralt, "Max Dickmann: el novelista y el hombre," *Revista iberoamericana,* No. 15 (1944), 49-56.

fiction of the period,[3] *Madre América* (1935) is neither denunciatory nor proletarian in its focus. However, what does make the novel of interest for an examination of literary attempts to contribute to the social consensus of Argentina in the thirties and forties is the way in which it provides a refracted image of the moral and ethical decline of the period as, in the wake of the institutional disruption of the military coup of September 6, 1930, all manner of opportunists struggled to gain a share of power in the new "nationalistic" state.

Madre América is a rather disjointed novel. Divided into two parts, *El río* (the first third of the text) and *El pueblo* (the remaining two thirds), it is essentially a mosaic of types and situations held together by a vague narrative thread that only emerges strongly at the end with the triumph of one contestant in a bid for political power in the small fictional town of San Itatí and the death from pneumonia of one of his opponents. The latter is a member of one of the old but impoverished families of San Itatí (i.e., the founding Creole stock), while the former symbolizes the parvenus who are the delegates of economic and political interests of the new military regime (significantly, he has a French surname).

Touching on the elements of small-town jealousies, pretensions, and influence brokering, Dickmann's text moves from the isolated life of small property owners along the banks of the vast Río de la Plata delta system into one of the typical rural towns along the Río Paraná that feeds into the delta. The novel opens with a poetic evocation of dawn along the riverbanks and closes with a similar evocation of sunset as it falls on the decayed walls of one of the town's buildings. This framing device signals the novel's pretense at a natural or representative cycle of events, and the mixture of the commonplaces of evocations of a *locus amoenus* with a *fleurs-du-mal* symbolism (for example, the sunset falls on a fly twitching in the web of an alert spider in the corner of the wall) bespeaks the novel's overall evocation of idyllic settings spoiled by the mean and ugly drives of the human types who inhabit them.

----

[3] Concerning the reception of Erskine Caldwell in Latin America, see Arnold Chapman, "Erskine Caldwell: a Failure of the Grotesque," in his *The Spanish American Reception of United States Fiction* (Berkeley: University of California Press, 1966), pp. 150-163.

These types include, of course, the contestants for political power, and their values, hypocrisies, and grasping opportunism are described in appropriate detail. But they also include the representatives of the old order, the venal and self-important village priest, the fleshy old maids and *beatas* who fawn on him, and the shrewd and grasping peasants who seek to derive advantage from the needs of the gentry. A final element is made up of young adults who evince the cynicism and amoral self-centeredness of a period characterized by social upheaval and naked power politics. Essentially, the only character who is presented positively is Gabriel, a young rootless nephew of the Creole who loses out to the parvenu for political influence. Gabriel returns to San Itatí, to the house of his mother's decaying family, after working along the river as a hired hand.

Gabriel serves to connect the two parts of the novel, and he is an important interior observer of events for the reader, although Dickmann does not develop this role for him to any significant degree. That is, Gabriel is considerably underplayed as the image of the seer-participant in comparison to Ramón Moreyra in Varela's *El río oscuro*. However, it is through him that we see the illegal contraband traffic along the branches of the delta region, a traffic controlled by the politicians and their agents of law and order, and he is tangentially involved in witnessing the grab for power when he decides to return to San Itatí. It is unfortunate that Dickmann chose not to give Gabriel a greater role in the second, longer half of the novel. His point of view in various forms could have served effectively to unify the rather rambling exposition that the novelist opts for in his apparent desire to render a detailed portrait of social corruption.

Dickmann's novel reveals two basic strategies for textual unity. One is the rather typical and costumary one of a unified point of view. The narrative voice of the novel is sardonic and ironic in its portrayal of the motivating drives of the characters, the mechanisms of the self-delusion, and the sharp contrast between their alleged ideals and their mean and base behavior. The very title of the novel is rather sarcastic, with its implications of a benevolent Mother Earth myth: the maternally anthropomorphized continent nurturing and caring for its inhabitants in the tradition of the mythopoeic Argentine writings like those of William Henry Hudson, Ricardo Güiraldes,

Ricardo Rojas, and, of course, Leopoldo Lugones, whose *La grande Argentina* had recently been published, in 1930. [4]

Clearly, Dickmann has no use for hypotheses about a powerful spirit of the land that infuses the actions of humble children of the earth with dignity and nobility in their pursuit of national destiny. [5] Such an ideology, whatever its legitimate origins may have been in Romantic aesthetics, served as a shibboleth of the nationalists, and it is significant that *Madre América,* with its rural setting and its evocation of some of the prime points of reference to this mythopoeic ideology, undertakes to represent the most unredeemed versions of ignoble human corruption.

As a consequence, the narrator's overall narrative tone is also sarcastic in its relentless representation of the social and moral landscape of a period that, in Argentine social historiography, has come to be known as the *década infame,* the infamous decade. [6] The following passage, the conclusion of the narrative trajectory of the novel (which is thereupon closed by the aforementioned evocation of the sunset) is typical of the allusions in *Madre América* to the prevailing values of the political power in the country as well as of the narrator's portrayal of the participants in the panorama of the novel:

> —Todo cerrado —observa Goya, y en seguida, pensativo—: el fin de una familia.
> —Por una parte ha sido una suerte, si no un nombre más que cae en el barro —reflexiona Cardós.
> —Y para nosotros un cargo de conciencia menos—. Goya parece pensar en voz alta.
> —Tarde o temprano ese descalabro debía producirse.
> —¿Por qué afirma usted eso?
> —Créame que tengo mis razones... Es inútil, mi mujer es una vidente; ella me pronosticó todo hace un año o más,

---

[4] The nationalistic ideology of *La grande Argentina* is examined by Dardo Cúneo in "La crisis argentina del '30 en Güiraldes, Scalabrini Ortiz y Lugones," *Cuadernos americanos,* No. 140 (1965), 158-174.

[5] I am here disagreeing with Kuralt's rather gutsy assessment of Dickmann's benevolent humanism in his novels. Although he is certainly not mysanthropic, Dickmann hardly holds an optimistic view of mankind, at least as evidenced in *Madre América.*

[6] I believe the term *década infame* was first used in print by José Luis Torres, *La década infame* (Buenos Aires: Editorial de Formación "Patria," 1945).

cuando tuvo aquel gran disgusto con las hermanas del finado
Garabentos, y las cosas se han cumplido al pie de la letra.

—Pobre gente; no deja de ser triste eso de...

—Bueno, no se ponga usted sentimental, amigo Goya
—le palmea en la espalda afectuosamente Cardós.

—Es que..., bueno; ya no quiero ser así, pero hay veces
que siento como si algo llorara adentro mío... y me pongo
blando..., naturalmente; eso se me pasa al rato; entonces
vuelvo a ser el mismo y grito y mando que da gusto...

—Yo atribuiría eso a un desgaste nervioso excesivo.
Cuando le venga bien dese una vueltita por mi consulto-
rio...; le recomendaré unas gotas, y se acabarán los llantos
adentros [sic] del pecho... La energía y el carácter...

Sus palabras se pierden al dar vuelta en una esquina.
(p. 272)

The other textual strategy Dickmann employs is one that confirms
the novel's emphasis on the disjunction between reality and ideal,
between surface appearance and inner truth, and between the oppressive nature of a corrupt society and the individual's feeling for
a lost or missing idyllic circumstance. Throughout *Madre América,*
there is a play on the verb *ver.* This play involves either its literal
vs. its figurative meaning, "to see" vs. "to comprehend" or the
distinction between concrete seeing vs. imagining. In the latter cases,
attention shifts from a direct ocular perception on the part of the
character toward a daydreaming or a fantasizing that reveals Dickmann's familiarity with modern psychological theories about the
interpretation of dreams and surreal or subconscious images. Virtually all of the principal characters of the novel engage at one time
or another in this form of disjunctive seeing. Of course, all are
presented as seeing, literally, what goes on around them and as
reacting to it as either detached observers or as affected participants
in the situations they contemplate.

On the occasions when seeing assumes one of these nonliteral,
nonconcrete forms, the individual may recall a happier moment from
the past, may experience a fantasy that reveals an inner and secret
realm of true meaning and feeling, may grasp the implications of a
happening, may contemplate an ideal situation that is an impossibility
under present circumstances, or may simply speculate about alternate
meanings for what is going on. This form of metaphorical introspection is one of the few opportunities allowed by the narrative for

the characters to engage in introspection or to experience any form of self-reflection and self-contemplation that goes beyond the narrator's sardonic recital of degradation and human vanity. These moments, however, are of crucial significance for the novel, for they reveal the profound differences that exist between what people are and what they would want to be, between how they act and how they might wish to act, and between a depressing social reality and more appropriate or redeeming human feelings.

For example, one of the women in the novel who is drawn into an extramarital relationship with the man who wins the struggle for power understands both that she is being used by him for his personal ambitions and that there is little to recommend the seduction she see taking place as though a detached observer of her own fate:

> La carta cayó sobre la falda. Sus ojos quedaron fijos en las flores grises del empapelado. "Raquel", él me trata siempre con la misma fría familiaridad —pensó—. (p. 239)

> Lentamente, como un viento suave que fuera soplando la arena en espirales, ella muy corazón adentro fue modelando una imagen distinta a la realidad, pero alimentándola con esas dos fuentes sagradas en la vida de toda mujer: el ideal y los sueños. (p. 240)

Raquel's lover's rival for political power, the scion of an old Creole family of the town and the man who dies at the end of the novel, experiences a fantasmagoric revery that is a premonition of his own death. He goes to the town brothel on a stormy night to rescue the prostitute with whom he has fallen in love, having heard that there has been a murder at the house. In the process, he becomes soaked to the skin and subsequently dies of pneumonia. Afraid that perhaps Tina, his lover, has been the victim, Garabentos experiences a foreshadowing of what he will find that becomes a visionary foretelling of his own death (the Sarracán mentioned in the passage is another contender for political power, an inlaw of Garabentos and also a bitter enemy):

> Se pasó la mano por los ojos... Veía confusamente un amontonamiento de gente en un vestíbulo donde sonaba un gramófono, velaban al muerto con música de baile, un vals insoportable, chillón y romántico, que se pegaba al oído como el zumbar de una mosca fastidiosa. Tina, con un ves-

> tido azul estrellado, ofreciéndole una copa llena de un líqui-
> do rojo, espeso y tibio como sangre. Caras, muchas caras
> grotescas. Un mulato de pelo gris, guiñando un ojo, una
> risa que arrugaba el cutis de las mejillas hasta parecer trapo,
> unos ojos brillosos en un rostro redondo y carnoso en el
> que la boca era una herida angosta y violácea, una flor roja
> de pétalos caídos en medio de una solapa. El grupo se
> abría en silencio al ritmo de la música y todos los ojos
> miraban la cicatriz azul de la frente de Sarracán, con la
> cabeza aplastada contra el suelo... (p. 220)

The grotesque images of this vision are the natural correlatives
of the banally monstrous human types that populate Dickmann's
novel. Although lamentably *Madre América* lacks the structural
cohesiveness that would have made it truly a landmark work of the
period, there is no mistaking the overall image of Argentine society
that is projected by the fragmentary mosaic Dickmann chose of make
use of. The vision of Nico Bermúdez, the aging journalist who appears
briefly in the novel but whose perspective is the one that most
eloquently summarizes Dickmann's own, provides the pessimistic synthesis of the sense of *Madre América*:

> Vio a los hombres como eran, agarrados a los viejos,
> sucios y falsos ídolos, al ídolo escurridizo y abstracto del
> poder, apuntalado por la burguesía materialista y frívola.
> Vio cómo los jóvenes, esa dudosa e indefinida generación
> que no ha aprendido todavía a llamar las cosas por su nom-
> bre, vivían en un mundo poblado de imágenes y visiones
> deshumanizadas, y que, como todos los perezosos, los que
> nada hacen proponen siempre lo más espeluznante... (p.
> 139)

With all of its defects, it is in these terms that *Madre América*
remains one of the most eloquent evaluations of the moral and
ethical decline of Argentina during the infamous decade of the
thirties.

8. CARLOS RUIZ DAUDET'S *EL PUEBLO*: SARCASM AS NARRATIVE TONE

> Las cosas que ocurrían sólo iban a implicar un salto en el camino. Un salto sin trascendencia, ya que en estas tierras ninguna fuerza osaría llegar hasta el fondo de determinados problemas. Nadie iría a trastrocar los fundamentos del orden imperante. (p. 36)

> —Yo no estoy solo. Yo veo que empujando hay mucha masa de pueblo. Por cualquier camino la clase desposeída llegará encontrarse a sí misma, encima de la clase explotadora. Y esto le dará un grado de conciencia que nadie podrá luego robarle... (pp. 205-206) [1]

Like Max Dickmann's *Madre América* in its use of a provincial setting, as synecdochal of a national social and political reality, *El Pueblo* (published in 1949 by one of the major houses dedicated to committed writing) by Carlos Ruiz Daudet (1901-) [2] betrays some of the characteristics of social realism that have most caused the exasperation of subsequent novelists and critics. [3] Invested with a

---

[1] Carlos Ruiz Daudet, *El Pueblo* (Buenos Aires: Lautaro, 1949).

[2] On Ruiz Daudet's fiction, see the essays by Raúl Larra, "Carlos Ruiz Daudet, la vida provinciana," in his *Etcétera* (Buenos Aires: Ánfora, 1982), pp. 137-144; and Jorge Curi, "Un ortodoxo: Carlos Ruiz Daudet," *Contorno*, Nos. 5-6 (1955), 51-52. Curi sees the novelist as an orthodox, and therefore seriously limited, partyline communist: "Lo malo de Ruiz Daudet es esa creencia en que el entusiasmo social — el entusiasmo por un nuevo orden social, ni tan siquiera la participación en ese nuevo orden — basta para crear hombres nuevos, sin defectos y de una pieza, con un ingrato olor a premios stalines" (p. 51).

[3] See the opinions summarized by Francisco Herrera in his entry on Ruiz Daudet in Pedro Orgambide, and Roberto Yahni, *Enciclopedia de la literatura*

rosy-glow sympathy toward the members of the *partido,* both those possessed of an unswerving allegiance and those who experience various degrees of attraction to it, defined in terms of a virtual Manichaean dichotomy between Good and Evil and, above all else, highlighted by a relentlessly ironic or sarcastic narrative voice, narratives like *El Pueblo* juxtapose a group of characters with socially acceptable lifestyles and world-views and a sweep of background personalities and events that serve to underscore the difficult but ever-optimistic struggle undertaken by the former.

The two quotes that preface this discussion suggest these two poles. The first is part of an interior monologue by one of the "owners of the land," a man involved in numerous shady business transactions based on bribes, blackmail, and fraud. Although he has little use for the various degrees of fascism and militarism that held sway in the governments of the thirties and forties in Argentina, he also categorically dissociates himself from the philosophy of social progress that underlay the campaigns of those he dismisses as "communists" and "extremists." By contrast, the second quote is spoken with unreserved conviction by, precisely, one of the individuals whom the wealthy landowner can so easily and cynically dismiss. It is the interplay between these two points of view in the novel that lends to it the nature of black-and-white social commentary that makes it seem so dated to readers of subsequent literature of commitment, particularly that writing that explores the many ambiguities and contradictions of various Third-World and contemporary Marxist positions (for example, the image of revolution in Alejo Carpentier's *El siglo de las luces* [1962] or the problems of commitment and action in Julio Cortázar's *El libro de Manuel* [1973]).

El Pueblo takes its name from a hypothetical provincial town in the province of Buenos Aires, some distance both from the national capital of Buenos Aires and the provincial capital of La Plata: Chivilcoy, Azul, Tandil are towns that might well have served as models for El Pueblo (the author is from Tandil). These are towns that

---

argentina (Buenos Aires: Editorial Sudamericana, 1970), p. 543. See also the comments by Fernando Alonso and Arturo Rezzano in their *Novela y sociedad argentinas* (Buenos Aires: Editorial Paidós, 1971), pp. 168-169. Germán García states flatly that "Es ésta *[El Pueblo]* una novela de propaganda"; in his *La novela argentina* (Buenos Aires: Editorial Sudamericana, 1952), p. 266.

serve as commercial centers for the sprawling agricultural and cattle holdings of the province, the traditional bases of wealth for the Argentine gentry. Like so many novels of the period, El Pueblo is a mosaic narrative, and approximately fifty characters and their interests, concerns, opinions, and tribulations are woven together in some two hundred narrative blocks that run from half a page to several pages in length. The setting of the novel is the mid-forties, from the Rawson-Ramírez (both generals) overthrow of the Castillo government in June 1943 to the end of the Second World War and the first emergent signs of the new major political force of the period, Juan Domingo Perón, who had already been in the Casa Rosada for three years by the time Ruiz Daudet's novel was published.

Indeed, the two political parameters against which the novel's favorably portrayed characters define themselves is the shifting conservative-reactionary coalition of the monied interests and the fascist ideologues in the armed forces and among the bourgeoisie, and the Peronista demagoguery. The latter is identified in the novel with only the most oblique of references and the only overt descriptor used is a few passing allusions to the political base of the local political authority who replaces the military commissioner: " ¿Conoce la novedad?... Leiva es el jefe del nuevo movimiento... y si Leiva es jefe descamisado, no sé qué queda para los pobres..." (p. 216). By 1949, it was indeed clear that Perón's government was basing its broad apolitical appeal on the cooption of the demands by the left for social and economic reforms and that it intended to impose some form of censorship — basically asystematic but occasionally quite effective — on criticism from writers and activists committed to the prewar left. This circumstance undoubtedly accounts for the obliqueness of Ruiz Daudet's references to Peronismo and his decision to place the greater emphasis of his novel on the denunciation of oligarchic and reactionary traditions in Argentine society, which was, after all, what both the left and Peronismo ostensibly had in common. [4]

One of the narrative strategies that accounts for major features of El Pueblo's overall configurations is the considerable ambiguity over political definitions. This may derive in part from the new rules

---

[4] For the flow of these events, see Julia Elena Acuña, "Guía cronológica," in Jorge A. Paita, ed., *Argentina 1930-1960* (Buenos Aires: Sur, 1961), pp. 13-22.

and strictures of political commentary imposed by Perón's all-over-shadowing government (particularly in the effervescent days of the late forties and Eva Perón's fabled Rainbow Tour of Europe on behalf of her husband's government and its programs); it may in part derive from the novelist's expectation that his reader can be counted on to identify readily the complex strands of political and social philosophy that characterized the governments (the decade saw no less than five presidents in office before Perón's inauguration in 1946) and their opponents.

Yet, whether readers can readily identify or not the passing references to competing political beliefs, there is one pattern of disjunctive values that is immediately apparent and that leaves no room for doubt: the opposition between the clear and selfless commitment of the "extremists" and the checkerboard of contending political forces that are only united in their respective self-interest and their repudiation of the goals of the former. The latter range from old line anarchists to traditional conservatives, from wild-eyed adherents of militarism and fascism to opportunistic capitalists who are cheerfully able to align themselves with whomever is in power to staunch but frayed "radicales" (the Argentine equivalent of democratic populism) who claim the majority of followers but suffer the greatest discredit and disarray in the arena of political power.

The facile but not uninteresting disjunction between these two spheres of political behavior and representative characters is based primarily on the development of the unmistakable humanitarian goals of the *partido* and the maze of negatively defined features that underlie the goals of the other competing forces. The array of characters, concerns, and events that make up the narrative flow of *El Pueblo* serve to confirm this abiding disjunction, which is cast essentially in terms of the optimistic determination of the representatives of social Good to prevail against the hosts of cynical and self-serving Evil. By the end of the novel, the former have established some measure of coexistence with political interests, although it is not clear whether this is the result of their acceptance by these interests out of resignation or enlightenment, whether it is because of the changes in the lines of political power that come in the wake of Peronismo (which sought to centralize government and its services in the same way that militarism and fascism sought to centralize its corrective influence), or whether it is a consequence of the ultimately effective programs of the *partido*. The novel may well want the reader to believe the latter, but it is characteristic of the defects of rhetorical conviction that color novels like *El Pueblo* that such a circumstance is presented as de facto rather than as the result of a meticulously constructed narrative logic.

Narrative logic is, of course, what is most absent in a novel like *El Pueblo*. But this is, we may assert with critical confidence, an extension of the narrative structure chosen. Many of the novels of social realism, in Argentine as well as Western literature in general, are characterized by a texture that foregoes the narrative logic of, say, the novels of critical and psychological realism. Many of Erskine Caldwell's novels, which are perhaps the prototype of social realist fiction in the United States, may have a loose plot trajectory; yet they are marked by the absence of anything like careful cause-and-effect plotting. I argue below that Varela's *El río oscuro* is built upon a precise narrative logic, the development of the protagonist's sense of the imperative of revolutionary action. But other novels examined in this study eschew it as much as does Ruiz Daudet.

The rapid succession of narrative fragments that provide a mosaic of the social life of El Pueblo stimulate the reader's sense of the complex array of political forces at work in the synecdochal town. The narrator's use of an indirect free style to explore both the private thoughts in addition to the explicit utterances and behavior of his characters is colored by an ironic perspective that asks the reader to gauge the selfless commitment of the socially-committed men and women of the town and to judge harshly the ludicrous posturings of the purveyors and exploiters of the time-honored politics of influence and self-interest:

> El diario de Cambaceres [a radical] insertó un artículo necrológico sobre Videla [one of the revolutionaries gunned down by a political thug], pidiendo que cesara de una vez la discordia entre hermanos. "La Tradición" [an oligarchic and fascistic paper] apenas dio por su parte la noticia, atribuyendo desde luego el hecho al permanente clima de provocación que se generaba desde la extrema izquierda. Debajo del sueltillo, seguía un macizo artículo de doscientas palabras, con el título *"Nuestros Remates"*, llamando la atención de los señores ganaderos hacia el remate anunciado en la página final.

> Y en toda la página final, la firma Salaverri y Berteche
> avisaba que por exceso de producción, en la estancia de
> doña Leonor de Hidalgo [the wealthiest — and absentee —
> landowner of El Pueblo] iban a rematar el mes próximo
> ocho mil vacas, vaquillonas y novillos de una sola marca.
> (p 172)

The use of parenthetical asides to the reader ("desde luego"), the
use of clichés that superficially define an ideological position without
analyzing it ("permanente clima de provocación," "discordia entre
hermano"), and the ironic juxtaposition between the brief obituary
and the extensive commercial announcement are all narrative strategies that enhance the overall tone of sarcasm wielded by the
narrator:

> Finalmente los ejemplos procedían de lo alto. El go-
> bierno no se preocupaba de reparar o castigar el anterior
> desquicio administrativo, fuese de la esfera mayor, de la
> provincial o el de centenares de comunas. Por el contrario
> se ofrecía el caso de numerosos funcionarios que coimeaban
> con los bonos de nafta, con el cemento, con las bolsas, con
> los vagones.
> —*La intención "de éstos" puede ser honesta* —reflexionó
> [González, one of the wealthy commercial wheeler-dealers]
> haciendo un paréntesis a sus propias ideas—, *pero como
> cualquier gobierno, desde que el mundo es mundo, tiene en
> su seno a gente deshonesta.* (p. 128)

If the italicized segment is the articulation of González's interior
monologue, the opening portion of the paragraph is an indirect free
representation of the train of his assessment of the political forces
at play; this train of thought extends over three pages, and it is
characteristic of the general procedure of characterization the narrator
depends on to make this point about the features of life in *El Pueblo*
and the honest vs. disingenuous feelings of its opposing casts of
individuals and human types.

El Pueblo, although subsequent readers have found much to
object to in its unabashedly facile treatment of sociopolitical forces, is
not without its champions. [5] Certainly, it is indicative of the lesser

---

[5] Larra, for example, affirms that "En sus novelas Ruiz Daudet realizó
lo que recomendaban los Goncourt: contar la historia de gente sin historia.

artistic accomplishments of social realist fiction, despite the general interest in the characters and their concerns the narrator manages to awaken in the reader. But more than anything else, Ruiz Daudet's novel is an example of the microcosmic approach of the fiction of the period, of the deployment of an overpowering narrative voice, of the often clever reliance on a mosaic pattern of narrative fragments, and of the denunciation of cynical social pretensions that extends in Argentine fiction back to Roberto Payró's Pago Chico narratives in the nineteenth century. In this sense, it is a novel of some typicalness for the period.

Pero también, llevado por su concepción dialéctica del mundo, quiso ser no sólo el testigo sino también el orientador, influir con su propia ideología en la vida y en la conducta de los hombres" (p. 142).

IV. PROLETARIANS, THE OPPRESSED, AND THE FORGOTTEN

9. ELÍAS CASTELNUOVO'S *LARVAS*: THE NARRATIVE STRATEGIES OF DENUNCIATORY TESTIMONIAL

> —Un guacho —concluyó—: ¿de qué se puede reír un guacho? (p. 41)
>
> Mientras los "cráneos" del reformatorio se devanaban los sesos para clasificar a los asilados con el mayor rigor científico como se clasifica a los yuyos medicinales o a los insectos portadores de enfermedades palúdicas, los celadores, ignorantes y analfabetos, que se habían adueñado prácticamente del establecimiento, mataban a palos a las criaturas al margen de toda clasificación académica. (p. 104)
>
> —¿Acaso yo creo en la salvación de estas almas? —proseguí, señalando a un cretino que se chupaba los dedos—. ¿Creo yo acaso que el ambiente las deformó así? ¿No ve que son almas sin almas, taradas de nacimiento? (p. 199) [1]

When Enrique Medina published his first novel, *Las tumbas,* in 1972, it created a monumental scandal; it was also one of the most commercially successful Argentine novels of the decade. The reason for these two facts lies in the impact it created by its forthright moral and social honesty: for the first time in Argentine writing an author had spoken openly and without euphemistic reservation about the

---

[1] Elías Castelnuovo, *Larvas* (Buenos Aires: Editorial Cátedra Lisandro de la Torre, 1959).

life of children in reformatories and orphanages. The title refers to one of these infamous institutions, and the narrative is basically autobiographical. The narrative incidents described focus on the violence, the humiliation, and the irreflexive cruelty that characterize the relations of the inmates with one another, with abundant descriptions of both the sexual exploitation of one child by another and the sort of underworld social order created by the inmates among themselves.

However, the overriding concern of *Las tumbas* is with the way in which the institutional authorities wield a form of degrading violence against the children such that their harsh interpersonal commerce is but a pale reflection of the sadistic forms of law and order of the adult world. Although the repudiation of the novel by "decent" readers focused on the authentically scatalogical language employed in the clinical descriptions of the various forms of violation, sexual and otherwise, on the bodies of the children, what is fundamentally repugnant about *Las tumbas* for any responsible reader must be the pathetical accurate representation of a hideous social institution. [2]

One of the logical forerunners of Medina's novel is *Larvas* (1931) by Elías Castelnuovo (1893-). [3] Like *Las tumbas*, *Larvas* is a first-person autobiographical narrative. But where Medina's novel describes the reformatory from the point of view of one of its inmates, *Larvas* is told from the point of view of one of the teachers contracted to educate the flotsam and jetsam of society that ended up in such institutions. Like *Las tumbas*, *Larvas* also makes socially significant points by implication: penal institutions like juvenile reform schools are dumping grounds not only for young criminal offenders

---

[2] Medina's fiction is analyzed by Juan F. Bazán, "Enrique Medina," in his *Narrativa paraguaya y latinoamericana* (Asunción, 1976), pp. 259-275; and by Bella Josef, "Enrique Medina, o tempo sem recuperação," in her *O jogo mágico* (Rio de Janeiro: Livraria José Olympio Editora, 1980), pp. 118-20.

[3] Born in Uruguay, Castelnuovo published all of his works in Argentina, where he was a prominent member of the Boedo group in the 1920s and of other major groups of writers and social commentators. In 1933, he founded the Unión de Escritores Proletarios with Roberto Arlt. Yet, despite his extensive involvement with the causes of committed literature, there remains scant critical opinion on his work. See César Guiñazú, "Contribuciones a la lectura de Elías Castelnuovo," *Boletín de literatura argentina*, 1, 1 (1964), 73-79; and Francisco Herrera's entry in Pedro Orgambide and Roberto Yahni, *Enciclopedia de la literatura argentina* (Buenos Aires: Editorial Sudamericana, 1970), pp. 129-131.

but for an entire range of social misfits, orphans, and abandoned children as well. All are brought together in this melting pot of human degradation. And like essentially all literature dealing with houses of correction, Castelnuovo's narrative is concerned with raising rhetorically questions on the nature of such institutions, their internal organization, the alleged vs. the real social function they fulfill, and the pitiful facts of the texture of daily life within their walls. Written at a time when many areas of expression remained taboo, Castelnuovo can only insinuate two fundamental premises that Medina was later to make quite explicit: the reader of *Larvas* must assume from one passing reference the nature of the sexual harrassment that exists among the children and the fact that "reform" schools function to warehouse any child rejected by his parents or who falls outside existing social structures.

Whether Castelnuovo felt disinclined or constrained by censorship (his novel was published during the second year of Argentina's first infamous, repressive military dictatorship) from discussing directly these aspects of his subject, the simple fact is that *Larvas* is a trenchant denunciation of a major aspect of Argentine society in terms of the materials with which it does deal. Divided into nine sections that are case histories of individual inmates (eight boys and one girl who was abandoned at the all-male reformatory disguised as a boy), the gallery of Argentine youth the author invokes included, in addition to various nascent forms of criminality and violent antisocial behavior, bastards, degenerates (presumably Castelnuovo's designation for aggressive homosexuals), the mentally deficient, aboulics, and other assorted misfits.

Because of the gap of fifty years between Castelnuovo's novel and present psychosociological categories, it is often difficult to assess the exact meaning of terms like *degenerado, imbécil, tarado*: these are colloquial Spanish terms — the latter is characteristically Argentine — that cover ranges of semantic meaning too broad to be considered accurate sociological categories. But despite the author's anticlinical vocabulary (in fact, as my second epigraphic quote would indicate, he scorns the classifications of the scientific specialists), there is no mistaking the nature of the charges he is contracted to teach.

By the same token, there can be little doubt concerning the social environment from which these children are drawn and the various forms of degrading abuse to which they are subjected both by their parents prior to their arrival at the reformatory and by the celadores, the guardians of order, after their internment. They are variously victims of incest, child abuse, abandonment, gross social/institutional injustice and of the incompetence with which the officials handle their cases and the hypocrisy that the same invested authorities reveal in describing their exalted social function.

In general terms, Castelnuovo's autobiographical narrator, although he reveals an appropriate level of self-doubt as to his own efficacy and competence in dealing with the awesome social reality he discovers upon taking up a position at the reformatory, is a censorious, scrutinizing witness to a well-defined institutional crisis — the incompetent warehousing of physically and mentally abused children — that he wishes to denounce to the reader. From the perspective of the author, the narrative task is one of utilizing adequate narrative strategies to arouse understanding and indignation in his reader, and my critical analysis will concentrate on the identification of the strategies that Castelnuovo elects to bring to bear.

Like so many novels of the social realists in the mid-twentieth century, *Larvas* transmits both a sense of outrage in the face of a scandalous social phenomenon and a sense of sentimental lamentation in the face of the suffering that degraded and humiliated human beings are obliged to endure:

> Entonces, Frititis empezó a revisarse afanosamente los bolsillos del camisón. Todo su cuerpo huesudo y desarticulado se estremecía de una manera espantosa. Los dedos de sus manos al contraerse parecían las patas de una araña. Por fin, extrajo un pedazo de lápiz y un trozo de papel, y dificultosamente, garrapateó algo y me lo alcanzó.
>
> *Señor Director* —decía el papelito—: *hoy me toca el güevo y no me lo dan. Me quieren matar de hambre. Tengo el estómago vacío. ¿Qué hago?*
>
> Después dejó caer nuevamente el belfo y se fue replegando exactamente igual que una tortuga hasta quedarse por completo enroscado como si hubiese entrado otra vez en el vientre de la madre. (p. 151)

Although the rhetoric of sympathetic sentimentality with which Castelnuovo closes the majority of his case histories seems emotionally acritical in terms of the aesthetic distance maintained by contemporary documentary narratives and various forms of social denunciation and committed testimonial, *Larvas* provides the reader with such an unremitting representation of the grotesque social order of the reformatory that there is little comfort to be found in the narrator's rather lachrymose epiphonema.

Certainly the most outstanding feature of *Larvas* is the autobiographical narrator as critical observer. Many important works of the period established such a form of scrutiny as appropriate to the desire to render an accurate if not impartial perspective on an immediate social reality. From John Dos Passos's journalistic panoramas in *U.S.A.* (1937) to Christopher Isherwood's highly sardonic "I am the camera's eye" technique in *Goodbye to Berlin* (1939) and from the clinical gaze of Erskine Caldwell in works like *Tobacco Road* (1932) and *God's Little Acre* (1933) to the scathing dissections of society in great works of "hard-guys" detective fiction like the works of Raymond Chandler: *The Big Sleep* (1939) or *Farewell My Lovely* (1940), fiction as a microscopic lens applied to social types and situations emerged during the period through the use of testimonial if not necessarily autobiographical narrators.

Castelnuovo responds to this potential of social fiction of the 1930s and 1940s by postulating a narrator — clearly, the projection of his own self-image as regards a formative experience of his youth — whose task is both to present the reader with an unflinching portrait of the degraded existence of a group of social, emotional, and mental unfortunates and to comment on it in such a way as to leave little doubt as to its significance.

This portrait, which Francisco Herrera has aptly called "tremendist" to refer to the abundance of grotesque details designed to provoke a profound impact on the reader, is effected with an entire array of rhetorical strategies that leave little room for doubt as to the texture of social reality being evoked and the condemnation of institutional structures the author articulates through his narrative. The combination of scabrous detail and sentimental feelings, the unrelieved incompetence of the entire system and its representatives, and the inescapable damnation of the inmates who, one after another (with only one exception), are destroyed by an institution designed to "reform" them are all major themes Castelnuovo's narrator dwells on both as his version of a specific circumstance and as, on the level of the text's creation of meaning, a system of rhetorical figures that define a particular narrative universe.

One of the narrative's especially effective strategies is the doubling of the image of the teacher: the narrator as teacher points both to his role in the social context of the reformatory as the hapless mentor of knowledge for a group of children incapable of learning for a variety of congenital and socially determined reasons and to his role as the source of social awareness for the readers of *Larvas* whom he is called upon to "instruct" in the facts of the marginal world he discovers during his tenure at the reformatory. The opening paragraphs of the novel speak both to the narrator's role as witness and to the infernal nature of the other world that he unsuspectingly penetrates, so symbolically located far from population centers:

> Yo sabía muchas cosas ya. La vida me había enseñado bastante. A menudo, rodando y sufriendo se aprende más que sentado en el banco de un colegio. No sabía, sin embargo, lo qué [sic] era un reformatorio de menores. Por eso, sin estar habilitado para ello, acepté allí con gran alborozo un cargo de maestro. Entré, como todos, en calidad de interno. El establecimiento se hallaba tan lejos de la capital federal, por lo demás que la internación resultaba obligatoria. Se necesitaban cuatro horas de ferrocarril para llegar a la estación del pueblo y veinticinco minutos de diligencia para cubrir la distancia que existía entre la estación y la colonial infantil. [...]
>
> De los mil niños recluidos allí, unos clasificados como delincuentes, otros como defectuosos, otros como abandonados, difícilmente se podía encontrar con quien se pudiese compartir los sentimientos más elementales de la especie. Tal era el estado de deformación mental en que se encontraban al hacer su ingreso al asilo. Pasaban por tantos focos de corrupción —el conventillo, la taberna, los calabozos, los depósitos de contraventores, la miseria— que cuando desembocaban en el reformatorio estaban ya completamente corrompidos. (pp. 11-12)

Although the narrator shows himself to be a scoffer of the prevailing psychological and medical wisdom of his day in the matter of mental deficiency and criminality, *Larvas* is structured in terms of a portfolio of significant case histories. This technique both lends credence to the instructional quality of the narrator and legitimatizes the critical scrutiny — descriptive, analytical, and evaluative — to which a representative array of inmates are submitted by virtue of their obvious typicalness within the institutional underworld they inhabit.

To be sure, the utilization of case histories in support of the overall image of Argentina as a corrupt larvarium corresponds to the frequent disinterest of the writers of social realism in composing complex narrative trajectories based on dense psychological profiles of unique human individuals. Certainly, the children studied by the narrator-teacher lack any particular uniqueness beyond the grotesque circumstantiality of the context in which they are called forth as yet one more instance of the appalling situation they represent.

As a consequence, the various inmates, who are significantly portrayed in terms of their metonymic nicknames (and the narrator comments on several occasions that it was often impossible to determine their real names, as it was also difficult to determine the actual facts of their lives before their arrival at the reformatory), have the rather allegorical quality of the Ship of Fools trope: one child typifies the congenital imbecile, another the pathological murderer, and yet another the psychotic personality disorder. Metonymic names like Pajarito, Trompeta, Mandinga, Guitarrita provide the titles for the chapters (only the chapter devoted to the mascarading girl bears a Christian name, Ana María, the subject of the last chapter) and serve to underscore the attention to types. Although the narrator may choose not to classify them in terms of prevailing medical and psychosociological opinion, there is little doubt that he nevertheless sees them as integers in a faceless panorama of social circumstance where individual biography possesses meaning only in terms of that overall circumstance.

It would be natural for the reader of Castelnuovo's *Larvas* to understand the particular institution he describes as synecdochal of society as a whole. There is a long tradition of reading literature on the abuses of institutions of social care and control as addressing itself to the correspondence between those institutions and society as a whole: Hernán Valdés's *Tejas Verdes; diario de un campo de concentración en Chile* (1974) articulates just such a parallel. [4] One cannot miss the fact that the violence as degradation the narrator

[4] See my discussion of *Tejas Verdes* in "Latin American Documentary Narrative," *PMLA*, 99 (1984), 41-55.

finds in the reformatory is an extension, perhaps an exaggerated one, of society outside the walls, and many of the children simply bring to their life in the institution the pattern of behavior that has been formed both in the home and in the streets.

Yet, one of the important rhetorical procedures Castelnuovo utilizes in his depiction of the horrors of the reformatory is a defamiliarization of the accepted points of reference on the outside. I have already referred to the opening pages of the narrative in which the teacher underscores how ill-prepared he was for what he was to learn in the reformatory, and throughout the narrative crucial circumstances derive their symbolic power from the jarring contrast between what one may accept as a normal part of life and the deficient, distorted, or degraded existence that prevails in the reformatory. The narrator, in recounting one of the few cases that have a fortunate ending, that of the abandoned Pestolazzi whose mother returns to take him away, speaks of the strangeness that the simple word for mother evokes in the emotionally bruised child:

> —Comprendé esto —intervine yo, poniéndome de pie y cerrándole el paso—. ¡Es tu madre! Vos decís que los demás comprenden poco, pero vos no comprendés mucho que digamos. Esta mujer que está aquí es madre tuya. ¡Enterate!
> —¿Madre?
> —Sí, sí —certificó con prisa la interesada—, soy tu madre! ¡Tu madre!
> —Y eso, ¿cómo es?
> Me dio un coraje bárbaro. Lo aprisoné de un brazo y lo plantifiqué delante de la mujer.
> ¡Mirá: eso que vos preguntás es así: —le barboté— esta mujer que ves aquí, aquí, mirala, bueno, esta mujer te parió a vos! ¿Entendés? (p. 38)

The narrator's relation with Pestolazzi is of particular interest. It is the first case history presented, the only one that turns out well when the mother, ashamed at having abandoned her son, returns to claim him, and it concerns the child with a more or less normal personality. Pestolazzi's distinguishing characteristic is his implacable and insatiable questioning about everything, and hence the special ironic force of the narrator's attempts to bring him to understand the meaning of the concept of *madre*. Pestolazzi lays siege to the frustrated teacher with questions that follow every explanation with a new "Why?," every demonstration with a new "How?" This particular case history in the initial position in the narrative enables the reader to gauge the teacher's frustration: as he discovers and attempts to explain the degrading environment he has innocently entered, Pestolazzi bombards him with insistent questions that oblige him to recognize the futility of attempts at rational explanation. It is a variation on the "Out of the mouths of babes" topos, and the child never allows the teacher to forget the latter's exasperated declaration that he cannot answer many of the boy's queries:

> Desde entonces, Pestolazzi, siempre que me veía, balanceaba la cabeza como un péndulo, y decía en voz alta para que yo lo oyese:
> —No sé... No sé... ¡Y está enseñando! ¡Hay que embromarse! (p. 21)

Castelnuovo has been called the Argentine Gorky because of the concentration throughout his writing on the "lower depths" of society: one only need examine the titles of his works like *Malditos* (1925), *Entre los muertos* (1926), *Carne de hospital* (1930), and *Tinieblas* (3.ª ed., 1941) to appreciate the legitimacy of this designation. His writing deals with a range of aspects of the national reality that, if they were rather successfully hidden during the enormous economic expansion that occurred during the first three decades of the twentieth century, became abundantly clear with the economic and political disasters of the thirties and early forties. To be sure, the distinguishing characteristic of Castelnuovo's writing was the adequate representation and interpretation of the lifestyles of marginal groups of the populace from the sympathetic, "committed" point of view of the narrator. Such a point of view tended to describe and evaluate rather than to record: much of the writing of the period was, to use Wayne Booth's handy disjunction, "telling" rather than "showing." [5] Yet, the advantage of the duplication of the image of the teacher in *Larvas* enhances the opportunities to portray directly because the narrator, involved intimately in his own personal story, is able to recreate his pathetic conversations on the one hand with

---

[5] In *The Rhetoric of Fiction* (Chicago: University of Chicago Press, 1961).

the inmates and his (relatively fewer) exasperating interviews on the other with self-serving and ignorant authorities.

An immediate consequence of the narrator's portrayals is the jarring contrast in sociolinguistic registers. The Argentine novel of the period was undertaking the full representation in its dialogues of the speech patterns of the enormous range of social types to be found in a complex urban society like that of Buenos Aires. In line with the sort of novelistic texture introduced by Arlt in the late twenties whereby characters drawn from the lower and marginal sectors of society spoke with more or less sociolinguistic fidelity and whereby narrators, by the same token, began to make unashamed use of the lexical and morphosyntactic peculiarities of Porteño Spanish among even educated speakers,[6] the works of literature from the thirties onward would seek to give the impression that characters were speaking with their own authentic voice without the need for the stylistically superior narrator to call repeated attention to their lapses from academic Spanish. Of course, one still finds in a book like *Larvas* certain words italicized, one way of calling attention to their degree of unacceptability for whatever reason, and occasional inconsistencies in the representation of the patterns of colloquial speech, such as the transcription of the morphology of the Argentine *voseo* (i.e., the second-person singular pronouns and verb forms).[7] But the important point is that the reader derives from *Larvas* a fairly accurate sense of the speech patterns of the social outcasts being described.

There are three dominant sociolinguistic registers in *Larvas*. The most prevalent one is the fluent journalistic style of the narrator, interrupted on occasion by the need to resort to exclamation points and emotional rhetoric in the description of his despair in the face of stark facts. This is a form of writing entirely consonant with Argentine journalism of the period, where the development of a professional laconic style appealing to a broad base of readers was

---

[6] See Raúl Larra, "Roberto Arlt y el lenguaje," *Macedonio*, No. 11 (1971), 65-73; and my "Arlt: The Maverick," *Review*, No. 31 (1982), 29-30.

[7] For a survey of this question, consult María Isabel Gregorio de Mac, *El voseo en la literatura argentina* (Santa Fe, Arg.: Universidad Nacional del Litoral, Facultad de Filosofía y Letras, 1967), and Rodolfo A. Borello, *Habla y literatura en la Argentina* (Tucumán, Arg.: Universidad Nacional de Tucumán, Facultad de Filosofía y Letras, 1974).

punctuated by the markers of an attention-getting sensationalism that sought to involve the reader in the emotional impact of the story. As I have already noted, the closing paragraphs of some of the case histories resort to this form of emotionalism:

> Es verdad que lo atendí con la mayor solicitud y que en más de una ocasión no dormí en toda la noche, pero también es verdad que me olvidé de pronunciar aquella palabra, no sé qué palabra, mas una palabra tenía que ser, con la cual, a lo mejor, mientras el pobre se extinguía en la enfermería como un cirio, lo hubiera vuelto a la vida. (p. 172)

It is clearly a question of readers' tastes whether epiphonemic expressions of sentiment like this one detract from the sober and unrelenting chronicle of degrading social realities; certainly there are abundant examples in American narratives of social realism that manifest the same blend of detached journalistic account with parenthetical expressions of intense emotional or sentimental involvement. The more important issue is the clear stylistic register maintained by the narrator in his portrayal of the details of his personal experiences in the reformatory and in his analyses of a significant range of case histories.

By contrast, the inmates on the few occasions when they are given the opportunity to speak — and when they can speak through the curtain of aboulia and mental disorders that cripple many of them for purposes of human commerce of speech — express themselves with the language characteristic of both the lower social classes from which they are drawn and of the various experiences they have had in their young lives of abandonment, street crime, and marginal existence. There are certain terms that recur as leitmotifs in the narrative, *guacho* (i.e., orphan, bastard, misbegotten) being one of the most prominent.

The vocabulary of crime, of psychological and physical defects, and of physical violence constitutes typical words in the conversations of the inmates the narrator records. Although *Larvas* comes nowhere near achieving the scandalous concentration of such vocabulary to be found in Medina's *Las tumbas,* where the lexical subcategory of sexual violation is synecdochal of the generally abusive nature of the reform school, the speech of the children in Castel-

nuovo's narrative was a sufficient innovation for the literature of
the 1930s in Argentina to constitute an effective strategy for
characterizing the nature of the narrator's charges. Note the following contrast between the colloquial phrasings of one of the children
and the "standard" language of the institution's medical officer:

> Luego de cada exploración, el médico declaraba:
> —De aquí no es. No tiene nada acá.
> —¿Que viá a tener yo? —refutaba el chico, siempre
> que el hombre emitía alguna opinión—. ¡Si estoy lo más
> bien!
> —Podrías tener una pelotita en el cerebro —le expliqué
> yo—. O en la espina dorsal.
> —¿Lo qué?
> —Un quiste encefálico...
> —No miaga reír, ¿quiere? (p. 132)

Finally, there is the linguistic register corresponding to the shibboleths of the administration and the official myths of education,
social reform, and beneficial institutional caretaking. The narrator
is merciless in juxtaposing the actual facts of life in the reformatory
with the director's pronouncements and the various mottoes that he
lives by and that he has had placed on the walls of the classrooms.
These phrases synthesize a self-complacent moral superiority, and it
is evident from reading the case histories of *Larvas* that they have
little to do with harsh social realities. The incompetency of the
justice bureaucracy, which hides its bungling behind legalistic jargon;
the scientific explanations of the medical and social work personnel,
who are fundamentally unable to deal with the complex physical
and mental afflictions of their charges; and the pious bromides of
the administrators, whose belief in reforming education is a blind
for an insouciant dissociation from their duties, are all features of
the other aspect of the social reality in which the narrator sees
himself trapped. The basically inarticulate mumblings of the inmates
and the high-flown clichés of the authorities are the two extremes
of linguistic expression mediated by the sober recounting of case
histories by the teacher-witness.

Fernando Alonso and Arturo Rezzano, speaking of one of Castelnuovo's later novels concerning human suffering, significantly titled
Calvario (1956), summarize the sense of this author's work as a
whole in the following terms:

¿Puede considerársela social a esta novela y a la producción novelística de Castelnuovo? Pese a los reparos que le alcanzan, como eso de no trascender el límite de lo doméstico a pesar de llevarnos a casas humildes y a imprentas insalubres, a lejanos pueblos olvidados por los gobiernos y a cárceles nauseabundas hechas para mucho castigo y nada de regeneración, la afirmación está más cerca que lo contrario. Este tipo de literatura enraíza en lo social por traer personajes que configuran un orden social luchando por hacerse conocer en su oscuridad y abyección. Este autor, como dijimos, inunda nuestra imaginación de enfermos y pobres, de tarados y pecadores, pero todos ellos como productos de un orden social equivocado. Es una manera de interpretar un resultado y de echar a todo un pueblo un error. (p. 96). [8]

Clearly, such an evaluation is directly applicable to *Larvas,* one of Castelnuovo's early works but one of his most famous. Dealing as it does with a body of material that is decidedly more sociological than fictional and from a narrative perspective that underscores the writer's own autobiographical involvement in the otherworldly domain he portrays, *Larvas* is an outstanding example of the censorious writing of the social realists in Argentina both as a personal declaration concerning one of the many open sores of the national body and as the trenchant characterization of objective fact. [9]

----

[8] "Elías Castelnuovo," in their *Novela y sociedad argentinas* (Buenos Aires: Editorial Paidós, 1971), pp. 87-96.

[9] Despite the importance I have attributed to *Larvas,* note should be taken of the fact that Germán García apparently does not consider the work "novelistic" or "fictional" enough to include in his comments on Castelnuovo in *La novela argentina; un itinerario* (Buenos Aires: Editorial Sudamericana, 1952), pp. 259-261. García does, however, underscore the autobiographical nature of much of Castelnuovo's writing. It would be appropriate to note how not all of Castelnuovo's works fit the social realist mold. Indeed, Castelnuovo fluctuated between the sort of sentimentalized writing on marginated classes of the Boedo group and the more revolutionary perspective of the social realists. In this regard, see Liborio Justo, "Elías Castelnuovo," in his *Literatura argentina y expresión americana* (Buenos Aires: Editorial Rescate, 1976), pp. 157-164. Also worthy of mention is César Tiempo's prologue, "¿Te acordás, Elías, qué tiempos aquellos?" in Elías Castelnuovo, *Tinieblas* (Buenos Aires: Editorial Convergencia, 1975), pp. 7-16.

10. NARRATOR-READER COMPLICITY
IN ÁLVARO YUNQUE'S *NO HAY VACACIONES*

> —Me parece que lo que usted se ha olvidado
> de contarme sobre tu vida es más interesante que
> lo contado. ¿Eh? (pp. 51-52) [1]

One would not be likely to make the mistake of attributing
outstanding literary accomplishments to Álvaro Yunque (the pseud-
onym of Arístides Gandolfi Herrero, 1889-1982). [2] Certainly, the
overall defects of Yunque's writing — especially the mawkish sentimentality of his portraits of the powerless and the dispossessed
(typically, children [3]) and the deus ex machina staginess of his

---

[1] Álvaro Yunque, *No hay vacaciones (otros barcos de papel)* (Buenos Aires:
Editorial Futuro, 1959).

[2] See the entry on his writing by Pedro Orgambide in Pedro Orgambide,
and Roberto Yahni, *Enciclopedia de la literatura argentina* (Buenos Aires: Editorial Sudamericana, 1970), pp. 636-637. A "human" profile of Yunque is
provided by Raúl Larra, "Conversaciones con Álvaro Yunque," in his *Etcétera*
(Buenos Aires: Ánfora, 1982), pp. 63-75. See also Raúl Larra, "Álvaro Yunque:
ficción y pedagogía," in his *Mundo de escritores* (Buenos Aires: Ediciones
Sílaba, 1973), pp. 7-14; and Humberto Constantini, "Álvaro Yunque, una acti-
tud," *La gaceta literaria*, No. 15 (1958), 3.

[3] See also the narratives of *Poncho* (Buenos Aires: Claridad, 1938). Yunque
pursued his interest in children's literature in an impressive list of titles. Of
particular note is his work of children's theater, *Somos hermanos (tres actos de
teatro para niños)*, which appeared in *Teatro del pueblo* [Buenos Aires], No. 7
(1936), 14-28. Of little interest theatrically (the same may be said about *Miguel
cantó [un acto de teatro militante]*, pp. 3-11 of the same issue), the play turns
on the confrontation between a group of children and a bully who intimidates
them. Accepting the proposition of the militant father of one of the children
that in unity lies strength, they challenge the bully as a united front and win
him over. Obviously, the children's experience in this conflict of day-to-day social
dynamics is a version in miniature of a political truism of revolutionary import.

plots — are not the lack of adequate experience as a writer. For, during the fifty years spanned by his books, Yunque tried his hand at all of the literary genres and left entries in all of the privileged categories of the successive movements that held sway in Argentina from the twenties onward. Indeed, it would be difficult to identify a more indefatigable writer during the period that is of concern to this study.

Moreover, Yunque authored the first comprehensive history of Argentine literature focused from the perspective of social commitment. But like so much of his writing, which seems today to be fatally flawed, even his *La literatura social en la Argentina* (Buenos Aires: Editorial Claridad, 1941) is of limited usefulness, precisely because it does not include any satisfactory characterization, either in terms of recognition or detail or analysis, of the concentration of socially-committed literature that one finds first with the Boedo group of the 1920s and then with the social realists of the 1930s.

No hay vacaciones, which appeared originally in 1935 and was reissued by Editorial Futuro in 1959, is probably as indicative as any of Yunque's literature of both his essential concerns and his strengths as well as his (unfortunately greater) weaknesses as a fiction writer. The title is logically incomplete, although there is a

---

The children echo the tropes of the father's militant faith (he instructs them by reading at length from *El apoyo mutuo* by Pedro Kropotkine), and their point of view is a framing device for scoring the points of that faith.

Both of the play texts are accompanied by explanatory prefaces that are declarations of social realist poetics. "Arte proletario" is the brief declaration that introduces *Miguel cantó*: "El arte proletario, es un arte militante, un arte-arma" (p. 2) is Yunque's unequivocal declaration. "¿Existe teatro para niños?" which prefaces *Somos hermanos,* is, however, of greater interest because of the uniqueness of the author's commitment to children's literature:

> Esas escenas fabricadas para hacer reír y de las que se extrae, inevitablemente, una moraleja harto manoseada, no tienen vida. Son cosas al margen de la vida, pertenecen al teatro, a la ficción, a lo convencional. No son arte, entonces, y menos arte para los niños, y menos aún *teatro para los niños* que si algo esencial debe tener, es realidad, veracidad. [...]
> El pueblo —instinto— acude al cinematógrafo como antes acudió al melodrama y lo aplaude quizá sólo por eso: Porque el bien triunfa.
> El niño no puede admitir otra conclusión. Para él, lo lógico es que el bueno venza al malo. Y este deseo íntimo del niño es el más íntimo deseo de la humanidad.
> Por eso, el teatro para los niños, teatro optimista, cátedra de valor y de amor, ejemplo de héroes, debe terminar con el definitivo y total triunfo del bien. (pp. 12-13)

subtitle, "(Otros barcos de papel)." [4] The notion of *vacaciones* logically presupposes a routine or quotidian circumstance from which one
can — or cannot, as the case may be — take a vacation: a job, an
educational setting, a repetitive situation or life style. In the case
of Yunque's work, the nine short stories make abundantly clear that
the nonexistent vacation alluded to is from the implacable cruelty,
misery, brutality, and inhumanity of the daily bread of life. This
human condition from which there is no recreative release is outlined
all the more vigorously and eloquently in these narratives by virtue
of the fact that all of the victims portrayed are essentially defense-
less children.

These young boys and girls, drawn from the comfortable middle
class as well as from the more disadvantaged marginal classes of
orphans, vagabonds, and children of immigrant laborers are not lacking in strategies for survival in the struggle for existence. But the
suffering to which they are exposed, a suffering that is as emotional
as it is physical, the result of both psychological and corporal abuse
in equal and intermingled parts, is portrayed as the prime metonym
of a dreadful and omnipresent human condition. The fact that these
youngsters are victims of adults who were once themselves children
is the awful truth of the social malaise of child abuse, which Yunque
seems to see as a fundamental human condition rather than an ab-
normal sociological phenomenon.

Yunque's basic strategy for achieving such a characterization
of the suffering of children is to imply an unbearable abyss between
the mental and spiritual world of his protagonists and that of their
parents, teachers, and sundry other authority figures. Moreover, the
entire narrative texture of *No hay vacaciones* is predicated on the
assumption that the narrator has a privileged access to the mental
and spiritual world of children, that he is in a position to contrast
and juxtapose it with that of the shoals of vicious or mindlessly
cruel adults among whom they move, that he enjoys through the
medium of his discourse a unique opportunity of communication
with the reader, and, finally, that the reader is predisposed (despite

---

[4] *Poncho* also carries the subtitle "Otros barcos de papel," which is obviously
Yunque's metaphor for children. Leónidas Barletta reviewed *Barcos de papel*;
cuentos (1926) in *Nosotros*, No. 211 (1926), 554-555.

the fact that they are both members of the adult world) to join with the narrator in deploring the facts of social life represented.

Each of the nine stories is a vignette around the theme of society's cruelty toward its children. In the title story, two adolescent boys are bonded in a Judas/Jesus relationship against the disdain of the Pharisees; the Judas figure, fulfilling unconsciously the task assigned him by school authorities, betrays the Jesus figure and then commits suicide. In "Choclo," a battered and mangy dog and a young boy are ranged in their need for each other's affections against insensitive and self-centered adults. In "La muñeca," a struggle for the possession of a doll between two sisters assumes tragic proportions against the backdrop of the heedless distraction and unthinking provocation of their parents. In "La cartera," a hapless youngster must undergo public humiliation and flogging at the hands of an ignorant father, whose tearful breakdown when he learns that his son has been wrongfully accused of stealing (perhaps the cardinal social sin in lower-class Argentine urban society) serves only to damn him further for his lack of charity rather than to exculpate him for his blind ignorance.

Throughout *No hay vacaciones,* the narrator implicitly demands that the reader accept as legitimate a voice that is by turns ironic, sarcastic, and condemnatory towards the children portrayed. Thus, the basic rhetorical strategy is to highlight, on the basis of these three intersecting tones and the various lexical features and narrative ploys they imply, the way in which children are over and over again obliged to be victims and martyrs of this circumstance of social life:

> Los otros chicos callaban [la verdad]: sus padres pegaban también. ¿Para qué exponerse a un golpe por expresar su sentimiento íntimo?
>
> Y lo escondieron, atemorizados, en sus almas. Allí su verdad dormiría muchos años, hasta que ellos fuesen hombres a su vez y pudieran hablar sin temor, porque entonces tendrían pies y puños para defender sus palabras. ¡Ah!; pero entonces, los puñetazos y puntapies [sic], habrían modificado sus almas, y éstas ya no tendrían como ahora, bien abiertos los ojos para ver la verdad, bien abiertos los oídos para escuchar la palabra del condenado, y comprender la inocencia, sentir la congoja del que padece injusticia...
> (p. 61)

This quote exemplifies many of the textual strategies employed by Yunque, strategies that function effectively for the characterization of the disjunction between adults and children and between other adults and the narrator and reader joined in a socially-committed complicity of comprehension. Yet, at the same time, what is at issue are also the strategies that sustain the high-pitched level of sentimentality and easy emotional response that blemish Yunque's fiction. There is an overwhelming rhetorical volume to the rights of representation assumed by the narrator that results as much in a loss of subtlety — i.e., the opportunity for the reader to reflect on the complexity of the human condition — as it does in the concentration of the one dominant note these texts strive to sound.

"Los grandes nunca pueden ver el mundo de los niños tal como es, exactamente, con todas sus maravillas y sus horrores" (p. 98). This is both the overriding truth of Yunque's narrative portrayal and the essence of the superior perception he attributes to himself as narrator at the same time he undertakes to share it with his reader. Toward this end, the number of recurring features coincide to sustain the rhetorical volume of *No hay vacaciones*.

For example, one can speak of the epigraphs that preface each of the stories: many are taken from prominent European authors — Tolstoy, Novalis, and the like — and at least one from a Latin American — the Cuban intellectual Enrique José Varona. Together they serve to provide a mechanism of confirmation for the points about the abyss of misunderstanding between adults and children that the stories deal with. Epigraphs predispose the reader to a specific attitude and ensure a specific reader of the narrator's tone or attitude.

The latter are, in turn, supported by markers that, beyond the transmission of information provided by the organization of the text into a flow of coherent discourse, are explicitly addressed to an implied reader. Such markers are the abundant exclamations and rhetorical questions that punctuate Yunque's writing. It is interesting to note that markers such as these are divided in their function. For, on the one hand, they are indicative of an indirect free style whereby the narrator captures the putative flavor of processes of thought and patterns of feeling of the characters. Yet, on the other hand, they are invitations to the reader to accept the specific rhetorical strategies, since the proper response to them is inherent in the text, and the exclamations are redundant to the extent that they only further stress the obvious sense of the situation being characterized:

> Lila habló. No sabía ella tampoco de dónde le manaba, como un manantial de agua caliente, el tumulto de palabras con que pretendía convencer a la madre: ¿Por qué sollozar? ¿Por qué no conchabarse? ¿Si la miseria había entrado en la casa y era preciso echarla de allí para que no estrangulase a los dos chiquillos, por qué no se uniría a la madre y, juntas las dos, sacarla afuera a empujones, a escobazos? ¡Fuera, la miseria, lejos, a la calle, a la casa los holgazones, fuera! (p. 73)

Certainly, such ploys leave little room for any ambiguity of meaning, and the narrator's self-assigned right to represent directly for the reader a secret consciousness of his young characters that is an unknown and hidden realm for the adults of the real world they inhabit is what provides the characteristic texture of Yunque's writing. Stagy and sentimental as these stories are, they provide nevertheless a clear portrait of a social circumstance of abiding interest to their author, who was one of the few writers of the period in Argentina to concern himself with children as a point of reference for a larger panorama of social ills.

11. ALFREDO VARELA'S *EL RÍO OSCURO:* STRUCTURING A REVOLUTIONARY CONSCIOUSNESS

> Y mientras tanto y a través de los años, y sur-
> cando este estremecido presente que vivimos, el río
> oscuro de la yerba sigue corriendo por el paisaje
> sudamericano, anega las ciudades y los campos, rea-
> nima e inyecta nueva aunque efímera fuerza a millo-
> nes de hombres agotados. Pero pocos de ellos adivi-
> nan que ese líquido verdoso cuyas burbujas rebosan
> su mate, esconde la pavorosa tragedia de los obreros
> encadenados allá en la maravillosa patria de la yerba,
> entre el delirio de la tierra roja y a la vera del otro
> río cristalino, el Alto Paraná, que, como la selva, lo
> sabe todo, pero calla y aguarda. (p. 240) [1]

One of the abiding features of the Latin American novel has been the symbolic representation of and coming to terms with a uniquely exotic landscape. [2] From the earliest representations of Nature in Latin American fiction, the chronicles which tended to translate specific features of the New World in terms of the idiom of classical allusions, down to works of the so-called *nueva narrativa* like Mario Vargas Llosa's *La casa verde* (1966) or João Guimarães Rosa's *Grande sertão: veredas* (1956), Latin American rural settings, particularly in the form of an exuberant and exotic jungle or in the shape of the haunting and mysterious *altiplano,* have constituted a preoccupation of writers as a cluster of themes that could be re-

---

[1] Alfredo Varela, *El río oscuro (la aventura de los yerbales vírgenes), no-vela*; 5. ed. argentina (Buenos Aires: Agepe, n.d.).

[2] Hence, Arturo Torres Rioseco's famous monograph, *Los novelistas de la tierra* (1941), subsequently issued as Part I of his *Grandes novelistas de la América hispana* (Berkeley: University of California Press, 1949).

presented as uniquely Latin American. In contrast to those strands of the novel in the nineteenth century or the early twentieth century that could be repudiated as, in modern sociological parlance, varieties of a dependency culture on the literary forms of the dominant centers — Romanticism, Realism-Naturalism, Vanguard Modernism (in the European, not Latin American sense of the term) — the novel of the land could in theme if not in technique of *écriture* lay some claim of varying degrees of sophistication to artistic uniqueness.[3]

Thus, although the narrative of social realism was to develop in the novel on topics relating to the exploitation of the *peón* as one of its major thematic features, these works superficially continue a significant inventory of titles that both describe the lifestyles of the countryside, so alien to the citydwellers who constitute the consumers of literature in Latin America, and lodge complaints with uneven eloquence against the abuses of first a feudal system of agricultural exploitation and then a foreign-dominated, capitalist machinery of intense profiteering. From Gregorio López y Fuentes's *El indio* (1935) to José Eustacio Rivera's *La vorágine* (1924), Latin American literature of the first half of this century contains a respectable body of works that approach this subject matter from a diversity of angles. William Henry Hudson's *Mansiones verdes* (1904; best known in English as *Green Mansions*) may represent one famous romantic vision of the Latin American exotic landscape. But the bulk of the titles that figure so prominently in this inventory both anticipate and fulfill the goal of the social realists to bring to the reader's attention the degrading existence of the peón and to stimulate an appropriate revolutionary consciousness.

Alfredo Varela's *El río oscuro* (1943) is undoubtedly one of the prime Argentine examples of this genre, and its translation into over a dozen languages attests to the interest it generated as a significant document of Latin American social realism.[4] The title evokes the

---

[3] Concerning the issues of dependency, see Jean Franco, *Criticism and literature within the context of a dependent culture* (New York: New York University, Ibero-American Language and Area Center, 1975). Its Occasional Papers, No. 16.

[4] There is very little criticism on Varela and his novel. See the dictionary entry by Francisco Herrera in Pedro Orgambide, and Roberto Yahni, *Enciclopedia de la literatura argentina* (Buenos Aires: Editorial Sudamericana, 1970), pp. 610-611. Miriam Curet de Anda's remarks are very superficial and, except

image of the flow of *yerba mate* — the ilex paraguayensis that serves as a national drink in Argentina, Paraguay, and Uruguay and is well-known internationally as a medicinal tea — as a surging, unbroken fluvial flow of green vegetation from the Alto Paraná to the population centers of South America's cone and then on to the international marketplaces. The story contained in *El río oscuro* has been told many times in the literature of the area, most notably and eloquently by Rafael Barrett, the Spanish-Paraguayan writer who first brought the plight of the *mensú,* the peón of the *yerbales vírgenes,* to the attention of a large reading public.[5] One also recalls the short stories of the Uruguayan writer Horacio Quiroga set in the same area during the early part of the century.

It is the story of the exploration of the peasant who is contracted to work in the primitive, wild yerba plantations with promises of fabulous wages to be earned. Once he arrives in the outback, often several days journey upriver from the nearest settled town, he discovers that he has already amassed a large debt with the (often foreign) company that has hired him for his clothes, for a modest

---

for details concerning the correspondences with Rivera's *La vorágine,* they do not rise above the level of plot summary: "El tema de la tierra en tres novelistas argentinos contemporáneos [Ernesto Castro, Varela, Juan Goyanarte]," *Ficción,* No. 38 (1962), 41-52; the comments on Varela appear on pp. 45-49. See also the pithy remarks by Jorge B. Rivera in his "Panorama de la novela argentina: 1930-1955," in *Capítulo; la historia de la literatura argentina* [2.ª ed.]. (Buenos Aires: Centro Editor de América Latina, 1981), No. 86, p. 326. Juan Carlos Portantiero provides the following, reservedly enthusiastic, assessment of Varela's novel: "Este camino [rural] dio logros individuales muy felices, como *El río oscuro* de Alfredo Varela, una de las mejores realizaciones de toda la literatura argentina, pero que al cabo, tampoco iba a la esencia del nuevo realismo, cuyo interés no deriva de incorporar como crónica los elementos fuertes de nuestra realidad, sino de integrar narrativamente lo humano-social, por medio de peripecias individuales desarrolladas en cualquier escenario. Esas novelas eran como grandes frescos periodísticos, muy atados a los modelos latinoamericanos, que durante la década del 30 marcaron los rumbos de la literatura social" (in his *Realismo y realidad en la narrativa argentina* [Buenos Aires: Ediciones Procyón, 1961], pp. 126-127). For a recent treatment of the image of the land in Latin American narrative — although works like Varela's are not mentioned — see Fernando Aínsa, *Los buscadores de la utopía; la significación novelesca del espacio latinoamericano* (Caracas: Monte Ávila, 1977). *El río oscuro* is mentioned only in passing by Ralph Kite, *Socialist Realism and the Spanish American Novel* (Unpublished Ph.D. dissertation, University of New Mexico, 1967), p. 59.

[5] See Rafael Barrett, *El dolor paraguayo* (Caracas: Biblioteca Ayacucho, 1978). Barrett's treatise was originally published in 1911.

advance (usually spent in predeparture revelry with prostitutes provided by the company and drink supplied by tavern owners on the dole from the contractors), and his transportation. Moreover, through creative bookkeeping and a complex system of demerits for "inferior" work, the promised wages never catch up with the debt, and the peasant finds that he has become indebted for life. In order to insure a proper level of production and to prevent dissatisfied workers from leaving the job, the owners have the work overseen by sadistic foremen who wield guns and fearsome native whips in the interests of no complaints and the uninterrupted flow of the lucrative "dark river." One should note that, while Varela's novel is the most important Argentine work on this subject, in Paraguayan literature Barrett's lead was to be followed by Augusto Roa Bastos, whose *Hijo de hombre* (1960) is artistically the most complex version of the subject. [6]

But *El río oscuro* is less important as an effective representation of the problem of the *yerbales vírgenes* (its subtitle is *Aventura de los yerbales vírgenes*). In fact, by the time Varela's novel was published the specific system of exploitation at issue, based on the ravaging of natural or wild yerbales, had already been replaced by the more systematic and labor-efficient cultivation of modern plantations on the fringes of civilization and under at least the nominal protection of enlightened labor laws. Although the internal evidence is sketchy, it would appear that the particular adventure related dates from the decade following World War I, and thus the novel does not treat a truly urgent question of latter-day labor exploitation, no matter how generalizable its theme is for the plight of the worker in the dehumanized capitalistic, feudal, and fascist society the social realists felt themselves constrained to portray. [7]

---

[6] David William Foster, "Christ Crucified as a Narrative Symbol in Roa Bastos' *Hijo de hombre*," *Books Abroad*, 37 (1963), 16-20; subsequently incorporated in *Augusto Roa Bastos* (New York: Twayne, 1978).

[7] It is interesting to note that, in an article published in the famous Argentine left-wing review *Contorno*, Noé Jitrik reproaches Varela's novel as adhering too closely to a doctrinaire, "foreign" definition of socialist commitment: "Los comunistas (Manauta, Barletta, Yunque, Varela)," *Contorno*, Nos. 5-6 (1955), 48-51. Jitrik writes that "No es, pues, *El Río Oscuro*, una novela americana, sino un intento, más ajustado que todos los presentes, de novela comunista o de un comunista bien de quien se guía por los principios del realismo socialista. Esto es del mayor interés. Hasta la fecha no sabíamos cómo

Rather, *El río oscuro* is immediately important to the project of the social realists in the period in which it was published for its representation of the evolution of a rebellious — if not specifically revolutionary — consciousness in the main character, Ramón Moreyra. Although initially nothing more than a young peasant more confident in his energetic masculinity than aware of the socioeconomic machinery in which he is one more human cog for the maximum profit of what the novel sarcastically calls the "pioneers" and the "conquerors," Ramón soon lives up to the heritage of rebellion evoked by his name, and Varela handles him as a contemporary encarnation of the legendary Juan Moreira, even more than Martín Fierro, the Argentine hero par excellence of the revolt against unjust and arbitrary authority.

Of considerable interest is the place of *El río oscuro* in the context of the Argentine debate between *civilización y barbarie,* the disjunction postulated by Sarmiento's *Facundo* which has served throughout Argentine sociocultural history as one of its major ideological axes. Certainly, Varela's novel concerns the brutalizing, "barbarizing," influence of life in a realm far removed from the urban locus customarily associated with civilization. But the jungle of the *yerbales* is both an anti-*locus amoenus* and a confirmation of the suspicion of refined Argentine city dwellers that the outback is a place of barbarian backwardness, and Varela's novel centers on how the *yerbales,* precisely because of the barbarous life imposed by a capitalism controlled by an urban-based economy, can engender a form of redeeming social consciousness.

As a consequence, the backbone of *El río oscuro* and the principal point of reference for the mosaic narrative fragments of which it is

---

podía trabajar estéticamente un hombre que en otros planos que los del arte representa una realidad humana incuestionable, que posee una personalidad construida en base a supuestos distintos y con apetencias y puntos de vista diferentes de los nuestros. Varela quizá sea el primero realmente bolchevique como novelista, por su forma de enfrentar las cosas y los seres. No que lo sea acabadamente (él mismo quizá no se lo haya exigido), sino que ofrece un modelo más ajustado, según el cual, sus hermanos de causa, más avezados, si existen, podrán guiarse" (p. 50). Jitrik is undeniably correct in his assessment, for Varela sees the mensús more as an oppressed lumpen proletariat than as feudal serfs. However, Jitrik fails to comment on the equally undeniable fact that *El río oscuro* is a far better novel than, say, the many American works to hew to a strict party line.

composed is the emergence of Ramón's understanding of the system
of exploitation he has signed on to serve and the development of his
decision to revolt against it. In the fashion of works of social revolution that exalt the attainment by heroes of their revolutionary
goals, no matter how partial in terms of an ideal program of social
structuring, *El río oscuro* concludes with the mensú's cry of victory
(significantly, in the Guaraní that is more legitimately the native
language of the peasants than the official Spanish or Portuguese of
their countries of origin) as he rides the waters of the Paraná river
to freedom from the almost unbreakable bonds of slavery at the hands
of the masters of the yerbales. I will discuss below the significant
interplay between the river of nature, the Paraná that carries Ramón
to freedom (as opposed to his enslavement, which is on board the
boats in the employ of the companies and against the tide of the river)
and the *río oscuro* of the title, the symbolic embodiment in Nature
of the whole system of exploitation and destruction.

Of considerable significance in the case of *El río oscuro* is the
person of Ramón Moreyra. Although Varela's novel has not provided
Argentine literature with a fictional hero that is immediately recognized by society at large (as Hernández did with *Martín Fierro,* Gu-
tiérrez with *Juan Moreira,* and Güiraldes with *Don Segundo Sombra*
significantly, all variants of the gaucho *typus,*) there is unquestionably
a substance to Moreyra that is often lacking in the novels of social
realism, where the main character is customarily an anthropomorphized idea. Certainly, Hugo del Carril's portrayal of Ramón Moreyra
in the film version of the novel (renamed *Las aguas bajan turbias*)
contributed to the general reading public's familiarity with *El río
oscuro* as the most famous novel of social realism in Argentina, and
del Carril's portrayal was facilitated by the particularized dimension
already present in Varela's script. Varela undoubtedly strove to invest
Moreyra with a depth of human pathos that transcends his simple
embodiment of a social hypothesis, and the drama of his struggle
against the river after his escape from the *yerbales* is told with considerable narrative intensity that leaves behind the reason for his
escape (a flight from grinding exploitation) to emphasize its goal:
the survival of the individual against overwhelming odds. This is not
to say that Varela falls back on the commonplace of Latin American
nature as the antagonist in the human struggle to survive, since it
is clear that the "dark river," although a blind and destructive force

of nature, is wielded by the agents of exploitation as an instrument in the social and economic exploitation of the individual. If a revolutionary ideal is personified in Moreyra, the capitalist system is objectified in the river against which he must struggle in his escape to freedom, and it is the conjunction of these two processes of narrative abstraction that lends particular resonance to Varela's character as one of the most outstanding human characterizations of Argentine social realism.

The growth of Ramón Moreyra's consciousness involves several stages of perception and a series of key incidents that represent the overall social reality of the enslavement of the mensús. Ramón is witness to the spectrum of details in the life of the mensú: the long hours and miserable working conditions in the jungle and the installations for curing and storing the yerba. He soon understands that the promises of the contractors who go into the towns along the river recruiting workers are accomplices in a vast network of shanghaiing, deceiving, and defrauding the worker and that the dire warnings of the few who have been able to return from working in the yerbales are indeed the strictest of truths. And most of all, he comes to understand the techniques of intimidation, physical abuse, and murder used by the owners and their henchmen to keep the workers in line. The yerbales are a hell without boundaries in which the mensú is condemned to slavery until he dies from exhaustion, is beaten to death, or is shot attempting to escape.

Ramón's growing awareness of his and his fellow worker's situation and the formation of a sense of rebellion is the opportunity for the novel to present a series of key scenes on the injustice of the system the mensú serves against his will. Thus, Ramón sees a man who has gotten drunk on the "generous" advance of the recruiter wake up to find himself tied up to a boat heading into the yerbales outback. He sees how the few men who take their women along with them (most are not legally married, and many of the women are tired prostitutes looking for an alternative to their lives in the small-town brothels serving the peasant workers of the region) discover that their women are welcome in the yerbales as occasional sex partners for the overseers. Ramón develops a primitive comprehension of the economic system of the yerbales, of how the mensú's expenses never are met by his income and how the overseers avail themselves of a complex system of discounts for allegedly inferior work or laziness to deprive the worker of his wages. Finally, Ramón witnesses the mechanism of violence that the owners have developed to ensure a steady workforce and a sustained level of productivity. The slightest infraction against the system, the most minimal gesture of defiance or rebellion, and the weakest sign of a letup in the rhythm of the labor force is met with physical abuse. This abuse may assume either the form of an abrupt attack on the spot of the offending worker or a calculated punishment staged for the sadistic pleasure of the administrators and as a horrible example to the workers.

Throughout *El río oscuro,* these key events and circumstances are depicted in terms of Ramón's understanding of how they constitute aspects of a system of exploitation and of how they justify his growing sense of angry revolt. Although the novel is not written exclusively from the point of view of Ramón's consciousness and despite the fact that there are many segments dealing with key circumstances that are not explicitly tied to his own experience in the yerbales, it is clear that of the gallery of representative men and women who appear in the novel, Ramón serves as the principal point of reference for the human tragedy being explained. Thus, soon after his arrival in the yerbales, he learns about how the women of his fellow workers are obliged to cater to the sexual needs of the overseers. In this scene, Ramón is the unwilling voyeur of the abuse of the woman who will later, after the death of the man with whom she arrived, become in turn his wife:

> El peón injuriado estaba junto al mostrador, donde apuraba vaso tras vaso sin acordarse de su mujer. Ahora era Ramón el que procuraba distinguir entre los bailarines. Pero no estaba. El ambiente era pesado e incómodo. Salió de la enramada, a campo abierto, y repentinamente quedó como ciego. La noche se le metió de golpe por los ojos, la boca, y los oídos, maternal e inmensa, inasible, impidiéndole distinguir objetos y sonidos. [...] Se adormecía, de pie, cuando lo empujaron. Salía una pareja. Él la tomaba del brazo, dominadoramente, mientras le dirigía palabras de oscuro significado. Ramón se despabiló, y entonces se dio cuenta. Él era el capanga [capataz] rubio. Ella, la mujer de Galarza. Parecía resistirse antes de llegar al rancho cercano. Pero su acompañante accionó con energía y los dos se hundieron en el hueco negro que dejó la puerta al abrirse. (p. 70)

Much later, when his sense of revolt against the many injustices he has witnessed has reached almost a fevered pitch, Ramón witnesses one of the many scenes of arbitrary cruelty against a fellow-worker that punctuate the daily routine of the yerbales. In this case, the Brazilian Frutos has accused the overseer Felicio of robbing him because the latter insists on discounting his work:

> —Yo trabajé y ahorita vos querés robarme mi plata... ¡Sos un ladrón, Felicio!
> ¡Ah, trompeta! ¡Tomá!...
> Con un salto felino, el contratista había salvado la distancia que lo separaba del hacero. Un rebencazo le cruzó el pecho y de inmediato un segundo trazó una marca sangrienta en la cara de Frutos. Quiso sacar su cuchillo, pero el tercer golpe certero se lo arrancó de las manos.
> —¡Tomá y tomá!
> Se dio vuelta y quiso huir. Encogió la espalda al sentir dos nuevos rebencazos que hicieron temblar su cuerpo alto y fino. Felicio aullaba como enloquecido por la persecución, poniendo todo su vigor en cada golpe.
> —¡Tomá y tomá!
> Al fin Frutos enderezó hacia la picadilla por donde había llegado Ramón. Como un venado herido se abalanzó desesperadamente entre las tacuaras y el ortigal, buscando eludir el castigo. Felicio continuó la persecución, arrojando el látigo para sacar el revólver. Como Moreyra, otros hacheros se habían acercado al escuchar los gritos. Siguieron al capataz encabezados por Ramón que llegó el primero. Pudo contemplar íntegramente el desarrollo del drama, que se precipitó en el espacio de segundos. (pp. 220-221)

It is this scene, which ends in the death of Frutos, who is allowed to rot in the sun under the tree that falls on him in his flight from Felicio, that results in Ramón's decision to make a break for freedom, but not without first killing the hated overseer.

In this way, *El río oscuro* follows Ramón in the full evolution of his need to rebel against and to destroy, in his own unaided and primitive fashion, one small aspect of the monster of exploitation of the mensú. Varela's text is, of course, not a psychological novel, nor does it strive for a mythic interpretation of Ramón as Roa Bastos does with Cristóbal Jara in *Hijo de hombre,* where Jara is a Christ figure whose personal sufferings and sacrifices are in the name of his fellow men. *El río oscuro* is not psychological or mythical vis-à-vis

the character of Ramón in the sense that there is no symbolic uniqueness about him such that he acquires a depth of complex meaning in
the course of his depiction.

Moreover, the novel does not really dwell on Ramón and his
consciousness. The narrative voice assumes many discourse forms in
El río oscuro, and only one of them focuses on Ramón. However,
what is significant is that Ramón appears as a point of reference for
the narrative when emphasis is placed on key aspects of the exploitation of the mensús. And, since one of the aspects of meaning in
El río oscuro concerns the need to destroy the system of exploitation
represented by the yerbales, Ramón figures prominently to articulate
this need as one man's reaction to his degradation within that system.

Ramón is — despite the force of his character — thus little more
than a lens through which the narrator focuses the major stages of
the narration, and it is important to note that this principal character
constitutes a doubling of the implied reader of the text.

There is, to be sure, no reliable way of determining who the
actual readers of *El río oscuro* were and still continue to be, nor who
the ideal readers Valera as a committed novelist had in mind. However, it is possible to determine the nature of the implied reader: the
reader to whom the various discourses of the text are addressed by
implication. [8] For example, it is fairly clear that Varela assumed that
his readers — most likely the large middle-class reading public of
Buenos Aires and the handful of other large cities in Argentina in
the first instance; the educated and interested foreign readers the
novel might appeal to beyond the country of its publication — had
only a sketchy idea concerning the yerbales. Hence, his text includes
not only documentary material from a wide variety of sources in the
form of epigraphs: quotes from the writings of Rafael Barrett, from
anonymous chronicles, and from signed personal accounts of adventures and experiences in the region. The novel also includes, under
the heading of "La conquista," ten brief segments in a highly fig-

---

[8] The term "implied reader" derives from the writings of Wolfgang Iser,
especially his *The Impied Reader* (Baltimore: Johns Hopkins University Press,
1974), where he develops the premise that it is the implied reader who is asked
to complete the meaning of the text. See also Jane P. Tompkins, "An Introduction to Reader-Response Criticism," in her edited collection, *Reader-Response
Criticism, from Formalism to Post-Structuralism* (Baltimore: Johns Hopkins University Press, 1980), pp. ix-xxvi.

urative or poetic prose that characterize the history of the economic conquest of the yerbales. Such material carries the implication that it is necessary to the reader in order to understand the historical and sociological context of the fictional narrative being presented. Put differently, this material would not make much sense addressed to a reader with a firm grasp of the background information it contains.

Furthermore, the implied readers of *El río oscuro,* we may safely say, have only a vague idea of the injustices the mensú is made to suffer in the extraction of the tea the former consume in such copious quantities. There are repeated references in the novel, most notably in the sections entitled "La conquista," as to how the yerba mate drinkers are unaware of the suffering necessary for them to enjoy the national beverage:

> Buenos Aires y Santa Fe se aficionaron al raro brebaje. Pasó las fronteras coloniales, atravesó en carretas lentas las enormes distancias, llegó a Chile, a Potosí, y a Lima. Y nadie sabía que ese gusto agrio de la yerba mate chamuscada se debía al dolor concentrado de los indios que habían caído jalonando la prosperidad de la industria. (p. 34)

This reference to the origins of the exploitation of the yerbales is complemented by similar statements regarding the ignorance of modern Argentines and Latin Americans surrounding the industry. The characterization of one of the most feared of the recruiters and overseers includes his recollection of a conversation on board one of the launches with an engineer, presumably from Buenos Aires, who explodes in indignation when he perceives the horrible reality of the yerbales beneath the casual conversation of the overseer, who has remarked on how it is sometimes necessary to hunt down escaping workers:

> Contra lo que esperaba, el otro se asombró, escandalizado:
>
> —¿Pero, cómo? Usted justifica el asesinato, entonces. ¡Es una barbaridad! Ahora veo que era cierto lo que...
>
> Mieres intentó calmarlo. Pero el ingeniero estaba indignado y se levantó de la mesa gritando:
>
> —¡Es una vergüenza que en la Argentina pasen estas cosas! ¡Después dicen que estamos civilizados! ¡Yo no sé qué hace el gobierno! ... (p. 174)

The engineer's sputtering indignation is a circumstantial example of the rage *El río oscuro* must create in the reader. His perception of the truth behind the rumors he has heard (this is the implication of the sentence he is unable to complete in his anger that it is true what they say that...) is precisely the truth concerning the yerbales that Valera's novel lays out for the reader in such overwhelming detail. And his final exclamation is certainly the question to be raised also in the mind of the reader as to how such social situations can be permitted in a country that calls itself civilized and that ostensibly lives by a code of laws to protect the individual from feudal slavery.

Thus, it becomes very clear what the nature of the implied readers of *El río oscuro* are like and what the demands placed on them are: they may have only a vague notion about the exploitation of peasant workers in the northern jungle reaches of the country, but they are called upon to sympathize with the plight of the mensú and to understand the need for social protest on the latter's behalf. The strategies of Varela's composition are designed to lead readers from a minimal comprehension of the problem to a full realization and sympathy with the human beings affected by it, and in this sense *El río oscuro* amply fulfills the dual objective of information and denunciation that so characterizes the novel of social realism in its exploration, for readers circumscribed by their rather limited social experience in bourgeois capitalist centers, of areas, strata, and features of society that they only vaguely know exists and have no basis in understanding to grasp critically or revolutionarily. [9]

Ramón as the lens for the reader focused on the social phenomenon Varela explores is, consequently, a rather ironic choice. Where other authors might use a narrator or character as focal consciousness, one who approximates the features of the implied reader (the first-person narrator-teacher of Elías Castelnuovo's *Larvas* for example or the detective-seer in Raymond Chandler's mystery fiction), the

---

[9] James Agee, in his book on Alabama sharecroppers, a book that has come to be considered one of the key documents in American social realism, states that his objective was to record the unthinkable: "Is what you hear pretty? or beautiful? or legal? or acceptable in polite or any other society? It is beyond any calculation savage and dangerous and murderous to all equilibrium in human life as human life is [...]" (in his "Preamble" to James Agee, and Walker Evans, *Let Us Now Praise Famous Men* [Boston: Houghton Mifflin, 1960], p. 16). Originally published in 1941.

reader of *El río oscuro* is asked, if not to identify with Ramón as the discoverer of a specific social reality, to accept his perspective as a legitimate window on the nature of his own experiences that the novel portrays as paradigmatic of the circumstances to be denounced. The unfolding of Ramón's consciousness of his own experiences, of his own "adventure" in the yerbales, is concomitantly the unfolding of the reader's awareness of a dreadful truth that has in general been concealed behind a veil of silence.

As a consequence, *El río oscuro* implicitly belies one of its early assertions concerning the plight of the mensú, an inherent contradiction that serves as one of the motivating forces for the privileged status of the text as revelation:

> Los muertos del Alto Paraná no tienen apellido ni familia. Y ni siquiera rostro, porque los peces hambrientos se los han picoteado durante el largo viaje, hasta dejar unas cuencas profundas, unos cartílagos temblorosos, un hueco inmenso donde antes hubo una boca que sabía decir palabras dulces y humildes o carajear borroscosamente. Los muertos del Alto Paraná no tienen historia. (p. 19)

This introductory assertion is triply ironic. Although as a direct statement of fact it is a metaphoric characterization of the circumstances of human misery and exploitation the narrative is undertaking to portray, as an introit to the narrative text it is a declaration that is ironically belied by the novel itself.

In the first place, the *muertos* do, in fact, have a story. It is the collocation of antecedents, details, allegations, and historical interpretations developed in the alternating texts under the headings of "La conquista" and "La trampa." Both sets of texts are differentiated from the narrative proper, the story of Ramón Moreyra's experiences in the yerbales, by their essayistic features. That is, they do not provide details about Ramón's experiences directly, but furnish background information as to the overall features of the yerbales, the system of exploitation, and the various historical details associated with it. They are also set off by the fact that the text of these segments is set in larger type than the specific narrative of Ramón.

"La conquista" places emphasis on the historical development of the system of exploitation, and "conquest" here refers to the attempts by the exploiters, whom Varela characterizes as Whitmanesque "pioneers," and to the triumph over the many adversities of the dense and turbulent jungle. The latter is cast in virtually anthropomorphic terms as a strong-willed defender of its own natural autonomy against the exploiters. On the other hand, the sections entitled "La trampa" focus on the various details of the system of exploitation that both ensnares the mensús in a trap of slavery and exploits the adversities of the jungle in sealing their death, as they are consumed by the all-devouring jungle in its struggle against the denizens of the exploiters. Varela, therefore, makes it abundantly clear that the Alto Paraná and its inhabitants do indeed have a long and complex history relating, lamentably, to the worst aspects of human slavery and degradation for purposes of personal economic gain.

But one might argue that when Varela says that the mensú has no history he is referring not to any lack of a coherent pattern of events surrounding his exploitation, but to the anonymity imposed upon him by the system that enslaves and destroys him. Yet this statement too is ironic and belied by the novel. El río oscuro is devoted to providing a reliable chronicle of the story of one representative mensú, Ramón Moreyra, and to informing the reader, whose sympathetic attention the narrative assumes it has engaged, as regards the details of his personal experiences as he enters into the realm of the yerbales, discovers the truth behind the reports and rumors he has heard about them, and comes to terms with his own determination to rebel against a life that he understands will otherwise end up destroying him. As I have already insisted, Ramón is both a figure of the collective identity of the mensús and a witness who beholds for the reader the horrible panorama of their lot. The specific details of his experiences in the yerbales and the scenes of cruelty and torment he witnesses are fragments in the comprehensive mosaic the novel traces. As a consequence, Ramón's story is nothing more nor less than the history that the novel's introit has denied exists for the mensú.

But there is yet another way in which the narrator's initial assertion is belied by the narrative text as the reader follows the steps in the evolution of Ramón Moreyra's consciousness. If the claim that the mensú has no history may also be taken to mean that he has not asserted his own identity and has not assumed responsibility for his own fate, accepting his own exploitation at the hands of the "conquerors" and resigning himself to the inevitable death assured by the struggle against the indomitable jungle, then Ramón's decision to rebel is a gesture in the direction of belying the mensú's lack of history. By responding to the rising anger he feels over the indignities he is forced both to witness and to suffer, Ramón is staking out for himself a bid to history in the guide of the social revolutionary spirit Varela's novel is rhetorically committed to.

Ramón's ability to evaluate his circumstance and to develop a feeling towards it other than the blind bursts of anger of his fellow workers, which merely give the overseer the pretext he needs to shoot them down in cold blood, is the nucleus of a sense of individual and collective history that makes *El río oscuro* a significant novel and not just another example of the denunciatory broadside in the service of political ideologies. In this sense, the following sort of meditation attributed to the protagonist by the narrator through the indirect discourse (i.e., free indirect style, as it is often called) that dominates in the novel is a particularly eloquent testimonial to Ramón's evolving sense of "historical" identity:

> Se inclinó [Ramón] para mirar entre el ramaje. Allá abajo estaba el contratista, ojos saltones, rebenque en mano y revólver al cinto. [...] Una vez habían matado así a cierto capataz, según le contaron. Pero Ramón ya había aprendido a dominar sus primeros impulsos y sabía reemplazarlos con una docilidad astuta y calculada. En la vida, todo sucede después de una larga preparación. [...] Cuando la sangre, que no sabe de tácticas, subía apresurada a la cabeza y alteraba su pulso y estremecía al corazón, animándolo a precipitarse, ahora Ramón sabía contestarle: todavía no. Ese "todavía no" marcaba los jalones de su humillación. Todavía no es tiempo de vengarse, todavía no es tiempo de contestar golpe por golpe, todavía no es tiempo de matar o morir. Todavía no. Esperemos. Todavía no. (pp. 139-140)

The ironic disjunction that exists, then, between the opening assertion, which is part of the narrator's overall characterization of the historical and sociopolitical backgrounds to the specific adventures in the yerbales of one individual that are about to be told, and the conclusions to be drawn from the narrative itself are hardly an internal contradiction of the text. Rather, this discourse strategy is part of the definition of the implied reader of *El río oscuro,* since an adequate reading of the text demands the way in which both the story as a specific text and the story as the literary representation of a specific human experience repudiate categorically the notion that the mensú is lacking in history. In this way, the history characterized on three interwoven levels by *El río oscuro* emerges as that much more eloquent as a consequence of this ironic framing.

If one of the significant aspects of the texture of *El río oscuro* is this ironic belying of its own historical postulate, another feature concerning its narrative texture also may be described as enhancing the reader's attribution of meaning to the details presented. Although Varela's novel accumulates a depressing array of details regarding the inhuman treatment of the mensú in the yerbales, the narrator frames these details with a register of expression that, in general and imprecise terms, we would call "poetic." The poeticalness of the narrator's articulation — and I have made a point above as to how he interprets, rather than transcribes, the protagonist's consciousness through indirect discourse that is an extension of his own distinctive mode of expression — lends an "abstract" or "mythical" quality to the narration as a whole.

The only significant exceptions to this univocal articulation are to be found in the epigraphic quotes attributed to other sources (some of which, in their turn, also strive for a suggestive poetic register) and the direct quotation of the speech of the mensús and their exploiters. Although the latter passages are in marked contrast to the narrator's voice and, in their occasional crudity, serve to remind us of the documentary commitment of social realism to the accurate representation of the marginal classes, *El río oscuro* is in no way a dialoguic novel or one especially characterized by the primacy of orality in the depiction of the revealing speech patterns of the lower classes. Varela is, to be sure, not alone in this regard: no Argentine novel of social realism comes close to the distinctive orality to be found in American writers of the period like John Steinbeck, James Farrell, or Erskine Caldwell; even William Faulkner's infamously convoluted, stream-of-consciousness syntax is capable of providing the reader with the flavor of the speech patterns of his characters as social entities. As the indirect discourse quoted above demonstrates, Varela's narrator cannot be said to seek such an accomodation.

The narrator of *El río oscuro* speaks in a "poetic voice" to the extent that his discourse accumulates a number of features traditionally associated with a poetic modality as against a fundamentally denotative exposition. [10] While the critic cannot define the opposition poetry/nonpoetry and must accept the impossibility of distinguishing categorically between connotative and denotative expression, between literal and metaphoric speech, an author strives for a sense of poeticalness by exploiting expressive strategies commonly or traditionally associated with such a register or range of registers. Thus, by using an elliptic syntax, by using both words that resist precise denotational meaning or which enjoy a range of possible overlapping meanings, by exploiting the cadences available in constructions that are syntactically parallel, by suggesting interpenetrating symbolic meanings through the use of phrasing like "as if" (i.e., A is as though it were B), and by highlighting rhetorical questions and exclamations to a degree recognizably excessive for "straight prose," the narrator is able to accumulate a series of linguistic features that contribute to a sense of poetic expression.

The anthropomorphization of the jungle is an outstanding example of these strategies: by investing the jungle with the features of an agressive defender against the exploitative encroachments of a human enemy, the narrative asks the reader to consider the metaphoric rather than the literal implications of what is described. For example, the product of the labors of the system of exploitation, the yerba mate, is described as a *río oscuro,* a dark river of green vegetation carried downstream but in stark opposition to the golden waters of the river of water that serves as the main road through the jungle. If the latter carries the mensú upstream to this enslavement in the service of the dark river, but also serves as a grave for his body after death:

> Un día, las lavanderas que bajan hasta el río amigo a desplegar el cartel multicolor de sus ropas, se encuentran con el hombre quieto y solo, junto a las piedras. Entonces se per-

---

[10] This distinction has in mind Roman Jakobson's definition of the poetic function in his "Closing Statement: Linguistics and Poetics," in Thomas A. Sebeok, ed., *Style in Language* (Cambridge, Mass.: The Technology Press of Massachussets Institute of Technology; New York: John Wiley, 1960), pp. 350-377. Although I know of no study treating the "poetic novel" as such, David Lodge discusses issues related to the examination of the verbal texture of fiction in his *Language of Fiction; Essays in Criticism and Verbal Analysis of the English Novel* (London: Routledge and Kegan Paul; New York: Columbia University Press, 1966).

signan y hablan apuradamente en un guaraní asustado y tembloroso. (p. 19)

That is why it is significant that Ramón Moreyra's successful rebellion against and escape from his enslavement is described in the three italicized segments as a "Galope en el río," for the "friendly" river now becomes the avenue of his escape from the dark river of exploitation and death.

Another way in which the narrator achieves a sense of poetic expression is by proposing a relationship of pathetic fallacy between the mensú and the jungle whereby the two entities assume interchangeable qualities and feelings. Thus, the sense of rage of the mensú against his exploitation at the hands of the "pioneer" is shared by the anthropomorphized jungle, which reacts against the rape of the conqueror:

> Al verlos aparecer (a los aventureros y invasores), la selva tiembla. Son sus enemigos. Sabe que desde ese momento se entabla una lucha honda y decisiva, a muerte. O ella, o los invasores. [...] La selva se arroja con su poder ancestral sobre las débiles carnes y la maltrecha voluntad de los aventureros. Puede asegurarse entonces que ya no llegarán a los yerbales vírgenes. Pronto da cuenta de ellos. Y entonces lanza un múltiple, alucinante grito de victoria, que comparten y repiten interminablemente sus animales y sus vegetales, todos los seres acogidos a su amorosa solicitud. La imponente madre ha triunfado una vez más, y todos comparten su júbilo. Por un tiempo —nadie sabe cuánto—, la vida seguirá como hasta entonces. Los invasores han sido derrotados. (p. 58)

The description of the jungle as an angry and protective mother and the representation of the encounter between the jungle and the invaders as a contest of opposing armies are metaphoric conceits that contribute to the sense of poetic expression. The reference to the yerbales as "virgins" that the mother will protect is an example of the play on a word of multiple meanings, since in the context of this quote it alludes to the image of the yerbales as daughters whom the mother jungle must guard against the rape of the invading conquerors, while to the latter the term virgen merely means that the yerbales have yet to be commercially exploited.

The characterization of the jungle as an avenger against the exploiter and as alternately the enemy of the mensú (to the degree that he is the instrument of the dark river) and his protector (to the extent that nature gathers back unto itself his lacerated cadaver) is one of the dominant features in the framing of the terrible plight of the mensú in terms of a poetic register that seeks to go beyond documentary detail to provide a mythic interpretation of the struggle between the forces of exploitation and the forces of nature. It is this struggle, with the cosmic implications of a contest between Life and Death, which provides the backdrop for the story of Ramón Moreyra as a prototypic mensú and invests it with a larger meaning than simply that of one individual's circumstantial rebellion. *El río oscuro* is one of the most significant documents of social realism in Argentina not just because of the extensive depiction it accords to the shameful treatment of the mensú in the forgotten outback of a country priding itself on its degree of European culture and sophistication. Rather, Varela's novel owes its literary stature in large measure to the complex range of narrative strategies the author takes advantage of and in particular to the way in which one individual's experiences are given resonance in terms of larger patterns of mythic and social meaning.

12.   A FEMINIST PROLETARIAN NOVEL:
JOSEFINA MARPONS'S *44 HORAS SEMANALES*

> —Esa es su labor, amigo mío; su deber de cro-
> nista: encontrar una verdad colectiva bajo nuestra
> elegancia individual. (p. 51)
>
> Los patrones ven en la mujer de trabajo una ac-
> cesible presa. Los compañeros, una enemiga que les
> disputa los puestos a cambio de menor sueldo. Ni
> unos ni otros adivinan el doloroso esfuerzo necesario
> para extraer de íntimas debilidades la fortaleza nece-
> saria para imponer sus condiciones de igualdad.
> (p. 100) [1]

The absence of women writers in Argentina during the period
of the thirties and forties is a curious aspect of the struggle for social
justice of the period. Although social realism in the United States
produced a number of women writers, some of them, like Harriette
Arnow and Josephine Herbst, of considerable note, one can say with
little fear of contradiction that this consciousness in Argentina — or,
indeed, in all of Latin America — was unable to count on the support
of a feminist or woman's point of view. During the period, the only
woman of international stature in Argentina was the Swiss-born
Alfonsina Storni, who committed suicide in 1938 in an apparent
emulation of Virginia Woolf. Only a handful of women are mentioned in Jorge B. Rivera's *Panorama de la novela argentina: 1930-
1955* [2]: Norah Lange, the only woman to enjoy a central position

---

[1] Josefina Marpons, *44 horas semanales* (Buenos Aires: Editorial "La Van-
guardia", 1936).

[2] Buenos Aires: Centro Editor de América Latina, 1981. Rivera's pamphlet
is No. 86 in the publisher's *Capítulo; la historia de la literatura argentina.*

in the vanguard poetry movement of the twenties; Silvina Bullrich, who began publishing in the early forties her fiction on the turbulent psyche of upper-middle class and middle class women; and Estela Canto, whom Rivera identifies as an example of "la novela de la ambigüedad" — presumably a variety of psychological introspection.

Of these writers, only Silvina Bullrich has established a major reputation, and criticism remains divided as to whether she represents an authentic form of feminist consciousness or whether she is but a competent writer of trite fiction for women.[3] It is only in the 1950s that Argentine fiction sees the emergence of an array of women writers who were successful both in establishing a secure foothold in all of the major forums for literature in that country and in developing a specifically feminist consciousness with its concomitant commentary on Argentine socioculture.[4]

For these reasons, and principally because of the derth of women writing in the thirties and forties on issues of concern to the social realists, to come upon Josefina Marpons's novel is indeed gratifying. Virtually unrecorded in Argentine literary history, this brief narrative is only 112 pages long in a very small format; the only mention of this novel that I have been able to find is in Fernando Alonso and Arturo Rezzano's *Novela y sociedad argentinas*. Regrettably, their brief characterization of it is incorrect in a major detail:

> Josefina Marpons llegó sagazmente hasta el visitado esce-
> nario de las fábricas en *44 horas semanales*, el vituperio de

---

[3] See, for example, the article by Corina S. Matheiu, "Argentine Women in the Novels of Silvina Bullrich," in Yvette E. Miller, and Charles M. Tatum, eds., *Latin American Women Writers* (Pittsburgh: Latin American Literary Review, 1975), pp. 68-74. A number of women scholars have written dissertations on Bullrich and have identified her with feminist concerns: Erica Marlene Frouman-Smith, Anna C. Tavenner, and Bobs McElroy Tusa. For a listing of scholarship on Bullrich, see my *Argentine Literature*; *a Research Guide*; 2d. ed. (New York: Garland, 1982), pp. 268-270.

[4] H. Ernest Lewald surveys women writers in "Two Generations of River Plate Women Writers," *Latin American Research Review*, 15, 1 (1980), 231-236. See also Dora Pastoriza Echebarne, "Argentina," in Else Hoppe, ed., *El hombre en la literatura de la mujer* (Madrid: Gredos, 1964), pp. 367-392; and Lee Roberts Shaw, "The Feminine Principle in a Masculine World: a Study of Contemporary Argentine Fiction by Women Writers, 1950-1970," *Dissertation Abstracts International*, 39 (1978), 1611A. Of particular interest is the anthology in English translation prepared by Lewald, *The Web*; *Stories by Argentine Women* (Washington, D.C.: Three Continents Press, 1983).

tantas mujeres que buscan, por detrás del camino del trabajo,
lo que éste no alcanza a darles por culpa de la codicia de
quienes, a otro precio, se lo entregan. [5]

In reality, *44 horas semanales* does not deal with factory workers
(which perhaps would have made it even more attractive, since such
a theme is paradigmatically social realist), but with office workers.
Office workers as a paradigm of victims of the dehumanizing forces
at work in capitalist, bourgeois Argentina are a common theme in
Argentine fiction, from the time of Roberto Mariani's classic *Cuentos
de la oficina* (1925) and Roberto Arlt's expressionistic drama *La isla
desierta* (1938), both works that reflect the interest in social themes
of the so-called Boedo proletarian writers of the 1920s. Office workers also constitute a social paradigm in the contemporary fiction of
the Uruguayan Mario Benedetti (cf. the Argentine film version of
La tregua by Sergio Renán) and in Ezequiel Martínez Estrada's
Kafkaesque *Sábado de gloria* (1944). The examples could undoubtedly
be easily multiplied.

Marpons's novel is a mosaic of Buenos Aires urban society from
the perspective of Camila Cellis, a young woman in her twenties
who works in the general offices of an unspecified company whose
owner, L. V. Perelli, is the prototype of the capitalist entrepreneur
who has made it on his own, married well, established himself in
Argentine high society and who manages his business with a combination of peasant shrewdness and patrician insensitivity and disdain
toward the "lower classes" who work for him. Arbitrary in his
dealings with the men under him and lecherous with the women,
Perelli functions in Marpons's novel as the embodiment of the social
system against which the female characters must struggle. Camila's
brother, Jaime, a shiftless introvert with pretensions at being an
artist, marries an heiress for convenience, finding success in a social
system that exploits his own sister.

Camila's experiences with the commercial marketplace and with
a family that abides unquestionably by the conventions of Argentine
bourgeois respectability (Camila's mother cannot understand why her
daughter cannot make her as happy as her son has done by marry-

---

[5] Fernando Alonso, and Arturo Rezzano, *Novela y sociedad argentinas* (Buenos Aires: Editorial Paidós, 1971), p. 131.

ing well) are lent a different register of support by those of her friend Aurelia. Aurelia too is an office worker, but she is also involved in militant worker causes, and her mother laments how her daughter's self-centeredness keeps her from participating cheerfully in the life of the household. Aurelia writes inflamatory pamphlets for militant causes, while both she and Camila sink deeper and deeper into the despair of a lifestyle in an indifferent society that promises little fulfillment for them and that, indeed, does not even heed their concerns. The coda of the novel is forcefully eloquent in summarizing the social mosaic it has presented. As two unemployed men, former acquaintances of Jaime, wander the streets trying to decide where they will spend the night, the narrator ticks off nine vignettes of what the other characters are doing at that hour:

> *A esa misma hora*
>> Alrededor de una mesa la familia de Aurelia comenta su egoísmo que la lleva a ocuparse de problemas que no los afectan de un modo personal, mientras aguardan al padre, retenido en la oficina una vez más fuera del horario. [...]
>
> *A esa misma hora*
>> Camila Cellis come en la cocina el pedazo de pan de que habla la Biblia. Tiene ojeras de cansancio y sueños; y sabe que el tiempo no se las borrará. [...]
>
> *A esa misma hora*
>> Aurelia proclama en un local desmantelado su fe en un porvenir más digno para la humanidad. (pp. 111-12)

The title *44 horas semanales* refers to the standard work week of the period, which included a four-hour stint on Saturday mornings (the so-called *sábado inglés*). The text is divided into four sections of equal length, "Ciudad," "Conquistas," "Sección presos sociales," and "Puntos de arribo." All of these titles are ironic in the sense that, contrary to a neutral meaning, they are invested by the narrator's scathing judgment concerning social exploitation and the destructiveness of an insensitive, dehumanized society. In the place of the romantic images of the traditional city (such as popularized by the culture of the twenties; cf. Borges's *Fervor de Buenos Aires* [1923]), the narrator dwells on the spiritual misery of households like the Cellis family and on the meanness of business establishments like Perelli's, where a male office employee who has complained about his wages is dismissed with the observation that a woman can be hired for half his salary, as, in fact, Camila is. Instead of commonplaces about making it in the world, Horatio Alger style, "Conquistas" concerns all of the elements that conspire against even the most minimal levels of economic success in the system; this section closes with the text of one of Aurelia's ringing diatribes, entitled " ¡Oye, mujer! No votan: los ebrios, los dementes, los analfabetos, y tú! " (pp. 63-64).

"Sección presos sociales" focuses, rather than directly on the practice at that time of sporadically imprisoning social dissenters and anarchists, often on trumped up charges, on how all of the characters of the novel are prisoners of a system of economic exploitation. And the final section is decidedly sarcastic in showing how the "points of arrival" of the characters are simply greater depths of despair, cynicism, and emotional atrophy. The irony of these headings and the sarcasm of the narrative voice provide an overriding coloration to the elements of the Argentine urban social experience presented by the novel.

If this dominant sarcastic irony provides the major principle for textual elaboration in Marpons's novel, it is reinforced by two other principles: the development of a fragmentary mosaic (so prized by the social realists) and the use of textual duplication. I have already alluded to the latter with reference to Aurelia's political tracts. These documents are texts within the novel that constitute one form of projection for the consciousness of the female protagonists. Each of the four sections of the novel is headed by an epigraph. Although these are not identified as being the words of anyone other than the narrator, they could well be Aurelia's also (the author's two-page introduction is prefaced by an epigraph from Jean Cocteau). For example, the following quote is the last half of the epigraph that opens the first section of the novel, and it echoes the sentiments of Aurelia's speech that closes the second section:

> Más allá del horizonte nos espera un paisaje mejor, pero hasta llegar a él es preciso hacer algo, cualquier cosa; hay mil clasificaciones: desocupado hasta ocioso; en ellas caben con distintos hombres los que van gastando jornadas de su propia vida en escalones de 8 horas. La costumbre impide notar a los hombres su propio esfuerzo y marchan con paso

tranquilo por sendas trazadas por ellos mismos. Pero las mujeres, que han tenido que correr para alcanzarlos, encuentran que la ruta es áspera y fatigosa. (pp. 9-10)

A different but eloquent example of textual duplication is the diary that Camila decides to keep. She opens it at the time she begins working for Perelli (who later fires her because of the repercussions of his own indiscretion in inviting her to tea). In it she records the humiliations and indignities of her job, the incomprehension of her family, and her by now routine engagement with another office worker, who always seems to lose his job before they can set a wedding date. If the fact that the novel was written by a woman provides a guarantee of at the very least an oblique feminine consciousness, the confessions to their diaries by the legions of drudges the narrator portrays provide an added degree of authentic representation.

44 horas semanales is "mosaic" to the extent that it is based on the conjugation of brief narrative fragments. The novel is uncharacteristically brief for the novel of the period (300 pages seems to have been the editorial norm), it is divided into four sections that stress a major perspective, each section is composed of narrative blocks rarely running more than two pages, and, overall, sentences and paragraphs are laconic. This fragmentariness and a tendency of the narrator to suppress transitional information result in an exposition of representative situations and events rather than a tightly-knit narrative trajectory based on complex causes and effects and psychological motivations. Such a textual pattern is appropriate to the novel's overriding interest in characterizing a general social situation rather than focusing on individual human histories.

As a consequence, Marpons's novel is based on a textual strategy of ironic juxtaposition, as the reader moves back and forth between brief characterizations of prototypic individuals and characteristic social circumstances. Camila, who is as close a main character as the novel has, is the hub of a series of digressive vignettes that may have the tendency to caricature types and situations, but which fit artfully together as a coherent image of a social reality. The rather tenuous plot line — Camila needs work, obtains it, and suffers the indignities of it, which include the insensitivity of her family — is a narrative pretext for the elaboration of the aforementioned mosaic of social reality. Marpons's novel is both pithy and eloquent. It evokes the texture of the absurd and cruel injustices of an arbitrary and dehumanizing urban capitalist-commercial society as it affects one of the latter's most marginal and exploited classes, women. In this sense, *44 horas semanales* is an excellent representative of the Argentine social realist project.

13. JUAN GOYANARTE'S *LAGO ARGENTINO:* EVERYMAN'S DEFEAT

> —¡Descansar...! En esta tierra cochina no se
> puede descansar nunca. (p. 52) [1]

Although considered a key Argentine novel of the 1940s and prefaced in its original edition by a very laudatory assessment signed by Ezequiel Martínez Estrada, [2] Juan Goyanarte's *Lago Argentino* (1946) is a difficult novel to fit into the context of an evaluation of social realism. [3] The foremost problem is the simple fact that it is not a well-crafted work of fiction, Martínez Estrada's judgement notwithstanding. A story of pioneer struggle, *Lago Argentino* is set in the environs of the actual glacier lake of this name in the southern tip of Argentina, at the foot of the Andes. There, Martín Arteche

---

[1] Juan Goyanarte, *Lago Argentino*; 7.ª ed. (Buenos Aires: Juan Goyanarte Editor, 1971).

[2] "Prólogo," pp. 7-10: "[...] levanta su obra a una de las mayores alturas logradas por la novela argentina, y, sin duda, hispanoamericana" (p. 10).

[3] There is relatively little criticism on Goyanarte's novel. Miriam Curet de Anda, "El tema de la tierra en tres novelistas argentinos contemporáneos," *Ficción*, No. 38 (1962), 41-52, provides little more than a thematic survey. It should be noted that the literary review *Ficción* was founded by Goyanarte in 1958. Juan Pinto, "Realismo y realidad en la obra de Juan Goyanarte," *Ficción*, Nos. 35-37 (1962), 101-111, provides a general characterizaton of Goyanarte's writing and a characterization of the "objective reality" of *Lago Argentino*. Jorge Campos also underscores the descriptive excellence of *Lago Argentino* in "Guiñol y realidad argentina: Juan Goyanarte en dos novelas," *Insula*, No. 191 (1962), 111. See the review by Carmen R. Gándara, *Realidad*, enero-febrero 1947, pp. 108-113; and the note by María Scrimaglio, "Dos novelas de Goyanarte [*Lago Argentino* y *La quemazón*]," *Boletín de literaturas hispánicas*, No. 3 (1961), 41-52.

works valiantly to establish a successful sheep ranch. Initially successful, in the end he loses out to It and to Them, rhetorically charged capitals that are in the spirit of the novel's rather intense deus ex machina narrative plotting. "It" refers to implacable nature, symbolized throughout the novel by the overwhelming presence of ice floes. "They" are the human flotsam and jetsam to be found on any frontier who are the nae — the thematic negative pole in semantic terms — of the noble Adamic figures who attempt to prevail, ultimately in such pitiful terms, against enormous odds.

Goyanarte's novel is a strange blend of the Argentine myths of telluric greatness and of the very concern of the social realists for the plight of the common or little man, and the protagonist is often perplexingly projected in both of these terms. However, despite the emphasis given to the superman, man-against-nature and circumstantial adversity, efforts by Martín to prevail against a hostile environment and an array of social circumstances that constitute an additive of adversity, *Lago Argentino* comes across as the other side of the coin of Leopoldo Lugones's protofascist *La Grande Argentina* (1930). Where Lugones was able to write of the transcendental imperative of Argentina to fulfill its manifest destiny within the framework of traditional oligarchic and agrarian values, despite his strategic admission of the many negative elements of Argentine society (the corruption and sickness, of course, that had resulted from straying from the path of the true and pure traditional values),[4] Goyanarte provides no comfort for the belief that the settlement of Patagonia will result from hard work, perseverence, and the commitment to a Creole ethic of camaraderie and fairhanded justice toward one's hired hands.

In the final analysis, Martín fails because of the falseness of the hope by which he lives. The entire constellation of adverse circumstances that he first believes that he can and has, in fact, overcome but which in the end preside over his devastating personal loss and financial ruin (his wife dies in childbirth at the hands of a medical impostor, and he is cheated out of his ranch by his duplicitous foreman) are, therefore, nothing more than the specific narrative

---

[4] The ideological bases of *La Grande Argentina* are examined by Dardo Cúneo, "La crisis argentina del '30 en Güiraldes, Scalabrini Ortiz y Lugones," *Cuadernos americanos*, No. 140 (1965), 158-174.

representations of the ironic disjunction between his steadfastly innocent convictions and the growing sense of impending and then
fulfilled doom that the narrator communicates to the reader. As a
consequence, the rhetoric of the novel demands that the reader take
seriously the disjunction between the lonely but idealistic individual
who demands the right to attempt to make it on his own and to
stake out a self-identity through the triumph of his undertaking.
(A novel like *Lago Argentino,* of course, defines its quest theme in
terms of an exclusively male undertaking, with only the most circumstantial assistance from women.) It is important that Martín is
of humble immigrant stock (his surname is of Basque origin) and
that he is assisted in his enterprise by a group of immigrants — a
Spaniard and a Yugoslavian — and by an Indian who is as much
on the margin of Argentine urban culture as are the foreigners, if
not more so.

Martín's social origins among the vast, only partially assimilated
late nineteenth-century immigrant stock and the petit bourgeois
background of the woman who will become his unstinting helpmate
bring *Lago Argentino* into line with so much of the social realist
or marginally social realist writing of the 1930s and 1940s. Certainly, Martín's identification with an entire range of cultural signposts
that fall outside of the ruling oligarchy (which has no presence in
the novel) or the dominant professional bourgeoisie (which is present
in only the most marginal and negative of terms, such as the impostor physician or the bureaucratic system that eventually deprives
him of his homestead unjustly) bespeaks Goyanarte's interest in heed-
ing the imperative of the period to focus on the forgotten elements
of Argentine society.

In the case of this novel, as well as of others that choose to
direct the reader's attention away from the primarily urban settings
of canonical social realism toward rural and provincial themes, if
not toward a specifically agrarian proletariat (the model of American
writers like Erskine Caldwell, John Steinbeck, or Richard Wright),
clustering the crucial points of reference for the narrative trajectory
around the image of a hostile natural force rather than an intran-
sigent social structure appears to be a strategic decision that high-
lights the noble struggle of the humble hero rather than a lamentable
turning away from the putatively overriding imperative to place emphasis on the details of an oppressive social structure. As we have

seen in the case of Varela's *El río oscuro,* the oppression of the mensú by an exploitative industry is translated equally in terms of threatening and destructive natural forces against which the workers must also defend themselves as though the latter were the agents of the exploiters.

The exploiters as an identified opposing force to the quest of the Adamic pioneers like Martín are absent in *Lago Argentino,* although the reader may wish to speculate, since no particular reason is given, as to why an entire range of marginal social types are obliged to foresake Argentina's much vaunted urban culture to eke out a living in decidedly inhospitable surroundings. Moreover, since so much of the bulk of the novel is given over to providing readers with background information concerning a part of Argentina — indeed, a vast nebulous hinterland — about which they have little reliable information, it may be assumed that the novel is fulfilling the need to contribute to the discovery of a large range of social realities that is one of the guiding maxims of the literature we are considering in this study. Certainly, there is no justification for the description of the etiology of glaciers and ice floes, of the dynamics of remote sheep ranches, of the demography of frontier settlements, or of the ethics of pioneer groups if such information can be counted as part of the common, presumed knowledge to be attributed to the ideal reader of *Lago Argentino.* The situation, of course, is quite the contrary, and the narrative implicitly complies with the discourse maxim to dwell on what is assumed to be "new information" for the ideal reader postulated by the text.[5]

The displacement of the opposing forces of overwhelming, hostile repression from a social entity to a natural one is undoubtedly the reason why Goyanarte's novel appears rather confusing in the context of the works of Varela, Kordon, Dickmann, and Verbitsky, and it is undoubtedly for this reason that it has been given rather short shrift

---

[5] Discourse maxims, which concern the implicit rules by which discourse takes place, is regulated, and grasped — discourse that is either literary or "colloquial," the former being a special, artistic case of the latter — have attracted considerable research interest. Two references of particular use to literary scholars are Mary Louise Pratt, *Toward a Speech Act Theory of Literary Discourse* (Bloomington: Indiana University Press, 1977); and Barbara Herrnstein Smith, *On the Margins of Discourse: the Relation of Literature to Language* (Chicago: University of Chicago Press, 1978).

in Argentine literary history. Yet, *Lago Argentino* is not without its own particular eloquence, and the representation of the elements that doom Martín's noble enterprise are presented in a matter-of-fact way markedly different from the rather overblown prose so characteristic of the "jungle" and *altiplano* novels of the regionalism of the period, a good measure of which can be found in Varela; Horacio Quiroga, likewise, is not without his lapses of purple prose in the face of an exotic, vibrant nature. The following is a typical representation by Goyanarte of the remote environment in which his forgotten social outcasts must survive:

> En algunos rincones de cordillera se ve el valle cubierto por los escombros de un trozo de montaña hecho añicos que se ha desmoronado de precipicio en precipicio, muy arriba, entre nubes, la montaña desgarrada que ha soltado aquel diluvio de peñascos; se ven también en algunos repliegues de la montaña rocas suspendidas en posturas absurdas que han quedado sujetadas momentáneamente por los escalones de piedra blancuzca. Se estira el cuello para mirar los desgarrones altísimos que acarician las nubes, los peñascos ansiosos de aplastar su base de tierra para lanzarse sobre nuestras cabezas, los escombros de todos tamaños que han surcado la pendiente con profundas estrías... El corazón se encoge. No pensamos que aquellos desmoronamientos tienen años, siglos quizás, y que es muy difícil que se produzca otro en los pocos minutos que estamos allí; nos envuelve la grandiosidad de aquella naturaleza salvaje, y se siente la depresión del cavernario agobiado por su propia insignificancia... (pp. 277-278)

Obeying the ideological imperative of the regionalism of the period for the narrator to serve as a reliable interpretive guide for the reader, the narrative voice slips easily from the impersonal third person *(se ve)* into an inclusive first-personal plural *(No pensamos, estamos allí)* that supposedly brings the reader into "direct" contact with the reality being described. In essence, the texture of *Lago Argentino* is a series of vignettes that characterize the frontier outback, the marginal social types that inhabit it — from the noble and enterprising Martín to a raft of unsavory individuals — and the precarious circumstances of their natural and social environment. Concomitantly, the information regarding the personal background of the principal, as well as of some of the secondary, characters allows for a series of mininarratives of social misfortune: the uprooted Yugoslavian soldier who saw the worst side of the Great War, the battered Spanish anarchist who takes leave to serve in the Spanish Civil War, the abused and betrayed domestic servant who commits suicide are some of the more memorable individuals portrayed.

One of the essential textual strategies in *Lago Argentino* is the adynaton expressed by the feeling that it would have been marvelous if Martín's efforts had prevailed. This adynaton is formulated more implicitly than overtly, but there is no question that the narrator balances his enthusiasm for Martín's project with an insistent representation of the odds against it:

> En esa Patagonia donde los vientos no dejan secar en paz los montones recién cortados, y donde muchos tienen que abandonar sus alfalfares cansados de luchar con los ciclones, el hallazgo de un lugar así era una bendición del cielo.
> ¡Cien hectáreas de riego! Hubiera sido magnífico. Potreritos de tres hectáreas bordeados de la doble hilera de álamos dibujados a tiralíneas. Canales, acequias, compuertas pintadas de verde. Un tablero de ajedrez con cien tonos distintos de verde. El triunfo de la geometría en el centro de aquel caos de montañas y ventisqueros. (p. 171)

However, there is no mistaking the heavy-handed ironic foreshadowing of the novel, as the narrator shares unremittingly with the reader the simple fact that Martín's dreams are doomed to failure despite their legitimacy and his innocent faith in them: "Y los esfuerzos humanos de Martín se asociaban al tiempo en un afán insaciable de superarse a sí mismo, de marchar hacia lo quimérico" (p. 174).

In contrast to the writings of the naturalists, wherein hospitable natural forces are objective correlatives of inherent human weaknesses and implacable biological motivations, Goyanarte's narrator expresses nothing but admiration for the nobility of Martín's enterprise. It is the inevitable outcome of the narrative trajectory and the basing of that conflict on the opposition between a sentimentalized, noble "little man" and the uncontrollable circumstances of his overall social and natural environment that allow us to consider *Lago Argentino* one variety of Argentine social fiction of the period.

V. CONCLUDING REMARKS

Contemporary Latin American literary scholarship agrees with considerable unanimity that it is an error to define the literary canon of Latin America in terms of the categories for describing European or American literature. Although one may acknowledge a dependency relationship between certain literatures and a handful of dominant models, to view world literature only in terms of the latter is to run the risk of ignoring a cultural production that may lie outside the scope of those models or to overstate the primacy of the latter in the formation of any one literary tradition.

In the case of Argentina, there is no question that foreign models have exercised considerable influence, and yet there are important segments of Argentine literature that cannot adequately be accounted for by reference to a privileged "international" model of which they may be local manifestations (e.g., the Gauchesque poetry of the late nineteenth century, the lyrics of the tango, contemporary socio-political/documentary writing, and the phenomenon of Borges).

It is impossible to speak of a group of writers related to social realism without evoking this question. For, if it is true that writers like Castelnuovo, Ruiz Daudet, Varela were clearly inspired by the doctrinaire principles of the Internationale of the period, others like Barletta and Goyanarte might well be accounted for without reference to as specific a concept as social realism. As a consequence, I have tried in this study not to insist on the need to define social realism in terms of Soviet aesthetics or in terms of highly prized English-language models. Rather, my use of the designation "social realism" is intended only to recognize that in Argentina, as in other Latin American countries during the same period, there is a block of writing that responds to a generalized Western commitment, extending back to the early part of the century but crystalized in the 1930s, to deal with the related issues of the identification of marginal social groups and the need for social justice.

Where the earlier Boedo writers of the period immediately following World War I tended to sentimentalize the depiction of the humble and the forgotten (cf. the general tenor of the lyrics of the tango, which have their roots in this period), the writers of the thirties were more interested in social dynamics. This posture is reflected in the more sweeping panorama of their writings (cf. Kordon, Scalabrini Ortiz, Barletta, Dickmann, Varela), where an entire social class and generalized social phenomena are of concern, and in a preoccupation with specific social ills that by extension — or by implication — can be addressed by programs of social and political action and renovation (Varela, Marpons, Ruiz Daudet).

If the writers examined in this study can be reasonably studied as part of a global commitment to the social issues of the day, in terms of the literary conventions and textual strategies employed in their writing one finds the constant presence of a controlling narrator who mediates explicitly between the reader and the social reality being described and analyzed. This strong narrator presence, and an attendant ironic voice in the face of individuals trapped in a social fabric they struggle to comprehend and to control, is a hallmark of the writing of the period and one of its unifying characteristics. Significantly, it is in Varela's *El río oscuro,* a sort of paradigm of social realist writing in Argentina and one of the most famous novels of the period, where the protagonist assumes an imposing identity that challenges the primacy of the narrator while at the same time revealing the heroic dimension sought for the exemplars of the struggle for revolutionary social vindication.

Of particular interest are the strategies for constructing a literature of testimonial denunciation, where the goal is to expose an ignored social reality. Castelnuovo does this in *Larvas,* and a significant procedure in his treatment of a scandalous institutional subculture is the use of a marginal vocabulary that serves to organize the depiction of the experiences that it registers. Rabinovich is concerned with portraying a marginal ethnic community submerged in the dominant mainstream, and a correlative of the margination of the members of that community is the narrator's overbearing expropiation of their voice: only he can speak for them in the mutism of their margination and dislocation. The same is true in the case of Yunque's children, whose physically battered and emotionally deprived existence leads to a state of disorientation that only the privileged narrator can compensate for.

The need to specify the parameters of the phenomena being analyzed — often with the implied assumption that it is for the first time — leads to a dependence on various rhetorical devices and procedures: the disjunctive patterns in Scalabrini Ortiz, the ironic questions and syntactic tags in Verbitsky, the impersonal predicates of Goyanarte. This array of phenomena, and it matters little whether we call them stylistic in conformance out of an interest in the particular idiosyncrasies of individual authors or textual strategies out of a commitment to an examination of the successive levels of patterns of semiosis in works and movements, complement the recurring themes of the writing of social realism and account for the specific literary features this study has been most interested in examining.

While the works of Argentine social realism have not attained any level of international recognition — few Latin American texts of the period have this honor — I have sought to show how they form part of a continuity with a global commitment to a literature of social(ist) commitment. Concomitantly, they are of a whole with the larger Argentine literary tradition, with the writings of the so-called Boedo group of the 1920s and with the literature of sociopolitical commitment that emerges in the wake of successive national crises following the collapse of the Peronista experiment. Indeed, the documentary texture of so much of the writing of the Argentine social realist is a reflection of the dominant professional involvement in journalism and publishing. This texture may have been repudiated by subsequent generations as lamentably "nonliterary" or "antiaesthetic," but it should be obvious that it has important successors in the sort of trenchant testimonial, nonfiction narrative that is an important hallmark of contemporary Latin American cultural writing. Seeing the literary texts of a Latin American nation that antedate current reader interest in exclusively recent titles as in phase with both global cultural trends and as constituents of the general and abiding patterns in the literature of Latin America is an important prerequisite to an understanding of the density of that literature as a whole.

The Department of Romance Studies Digital Arts and Collaboration Lab at the University of North Carolina at Chapel Hill is proud to support the digitization of the North Carolina Studies in the Romance Languages and Literatures series.

DEPARTMENT OF
Romance
Studies
Digital Arts and Collaboration Lab